BFI Film Classics

The BFI Film Classics is a series of books that introduces, interprets and celebrates landmarks of world cinema. Each volume offers an argument for the film's 'classic' status, together with discussion of its production and reception history, its place within a genre or national cinema, an account of its technical and aesthetic importance, and in many cases, the author's personal response to the film.

For a full list of titles available in the series, please visit our website: www.palgrave.com/bfi

'Magnificently concentrated examples of flowing freeform critical poetry.'
Uncut

'A formidable body of work collectively generating some fascinating insights into the evolution of cinema.'
Times Higher Education Supplement

'The series is a landmark in film criticism.'
Quarterly Review of Film and Video

'Possibly the most bountiful book series in the history of film criticism.'
Jonathan Rosenbaum, *Film Comment*

The Man Who Knew Too Much

Murray Pomerance

A BFI book published by Palgrave

First published in 2016 by
PALGRAVE

on behalf of the

BRITISH FILM INSTITUTE
21 Stephen Street, London W1T 1LN
www.bfi.org.uk

There's more to discover about film and television through the BFI. Our world-renowned archive, cinemas, festivals, films, publications and learning resources are here to inspire you.

Palgrave in the UK is an imprint of Macmillan Publishers Limited, registered in England, company number 785998, of 4 Crinan Street, London N1 9XW. Palgrave® and Macmillan® are registered trademarks in the United States, the United Kingdom, Europe and other countries.

Series cover design: Ashley Western
Series text design: ketchup/SE14
Images from *The Man Who Knew Too Much* (Alfred Hitchcock, 1956), © Paramount Pictures; *Rebecca* (Alfred Hitchcock, 1940), Selznick International Pictures. Images on pp. 12, 17, 18, 29, 30, 32, 34, 39, 45 (bottom), 49 (bottom), 58, 59, 67, courtesy of the Academy of Motion Picture Arts and Sciences

Set by Integra Software Services Pvt., Pondicherry, India
Printed in China

This book is printed on paper suitable for recycling and made from fully managed and sustained forest sources. Logging, pulping and manufacturing processes are expected to conform to the environmental regulations of the country of origin.

British Library Cataloguing-in-Publication Data
A catalogue record for this book is available from the British Library
A catalog record for this book is available from the Library of Congress

ISBN 978–1–84457–955–6

Contents

Acknowledgments

The production of this book was supported by the Office of the Dean of Arts, Ryerson University. I am indebted to a very large group of friends, associates, and strangers who recognised, in various ways, that there are moments in life when we all need a little help. My sincere thanks to the charming staff of Palgrave/BFI, including Nicola Cattini, Philippa Hudson, Charlotte Padmore, Jenna Steventon, Georgia Walters, Jennifer Winders, and this book's gifted designer Sophia Contento. The staff of the Margaret Herrick Library of the Academy of Motion Picture Arts and Sciences in Beverly Hills has been gracious and generous on this particular project for more than twenty years: my thanks to Val Almendariz, Clare Denk, Kathleen Dimpfl, Sam Gill, Christina Ha, Louise Hilton, Linda Harris Mehr, Barbara Hall, Jenny Romero, Matt Severson, and Faye Thompson. For considerable help, my gratitude – belated in all cases – also to Rosemary Ashbee, Peter Bogdanovich, Bob Bornstein, Abdelwahed Boutahor, Chris Buck, Henry Bumstead, Jane Callen, Brian Carr, May Castlebury, Graham Clarke, Herbert Coleman, Julie Compton, Ned Comstock, Saul Cooper, Rev. Sheila Coughtrey, Doris Day, Tom de Mary, Steven de Rosa, Lise Desablé, David Desser, Michael Doleschell, Vernon Duker, 'Doc' Erickson, Carl Forest, Dr Marty Frankel, Daniel Gélin, Lydie Gélin, Larry Germain, Dermot Grice, Bill Hansard, Mary Hayenga, John Michael Hayes, Irene Hayman, Dave Heath, Bruce Henderson, Joseph Herl, Norman N. Holland, Christopher Husted, Robin Jackson, Susan Johnson, Mai H. Kelton, Abdel Khalig Ali, Bill Krohn, Erinna Laffey, Susan Larocque, Don Larsson, Leonard Leff, Nina Leibman, Jay Livingston, Edward Maeder, Bernard S. Massey, Suzanne Meyers-Sawa, Dennis Mock, Ken Mogg, Cheryl Monk, James Naremore, Doug Nicholson, Christopher Olsen, Donna and Todd Optican, Pat Perilli, Felicity Pickup, Jeannie Pool, Janet I. Reese, Peggy Robertson, William Rothman, Adam Schachter, Marty Silver, Godfrey Smith, Steven

C. Smith, Leonard South, Gene Stavis, James Stevenson, Randy Talmadge, Nicholas Temperley, Jamie Thompson, Steve Veal, Eldridge Walker, John Waxman, Vicky and Patrick Weil, Elisabeth Weis, Caroline Wheeler, Dr David White, Steven Woodward, and David Wyndham-Lewis. Nellie Perret and Ariel Pomerance have given, without pause, the incalculable support of love.

Prefatory

I have been thinking about *The Man Who Knew Too Much* on and off for almost sixty years, since seeing it at the age of ten in 1956. Its riddles have become steadily more elaborate and twisting for me, the profundities deeper and more lambent. I have spoken with a large number of the people who helped Hitchcock make this film, both on camera (Doris Day, Daniel Gélin, Christopher Olsen) and in the dense behind-the-scenes territory (Henry Bumstead, Herbert Coleman, 'Doc' Erickson, John Michael Hayes, Jay Livingston, Leonard South), as well as researching the production files and communicating with numerous sources about location and musical work in London. Two points should be made about my general approach. First, scholarly criticism has generally failed to see the greatest philosophical considerations of the film, thinking of it rather superficially as a simple family melodrama starring a pop singer and a Hollywood legend; and further, almost all published critiques of the film – including Robin Wood's brilliant chapter in *Hitchcock's Films Revisited* – misread elements of the story so as to place the climax at the wrong point and to mark a resolution in what I take to be the wrong terms. This book is intended as a course corrective for those who sail the Hitchcockian seas. Second, I intentionally make almost no mention of the first (1934) version of this story, which Hitchcock himself considered weaker. It seems to me that a man of his intelligence and capacity would seek to remake a film only if the early version had no persisting value for him; but more, he in fact told his screenwriter, John Michael Hayes, *not* to watch the original film or engage with it in any way. The 1956 film stands on its own, notwithstanding some interesting points of comparison. My overriding tenet in writing this book is taken from a comment of François Truffaut's in 'Un Trousseau de fausses clés' (*Cahiers du cinéma* vol. 39, October 1954): 'The most honest response one can give an author or filmmaker is to try to know his book or film as well as he does.' With Hitchcock, I believe this is the path that offers the most light.

'Je m'excuse, mais …' ('Pardon me, but …')

The Story

Young Hank McKenna is kidnapped while vacationing in Marrakech with his parents, Ben and Jo. Anguished and now embroiled in an assassination plot to be carried out in London, they fly there to find the child, and experience a chain of fascinating but misleading adventures in their search. During a gala concert at the Royal Albert Hall, Jo's loss of composure happens to foil the planned murder, her scream throwing off the shooter's aim at the critical moment. She and Ben are invited to the intended victim's embassy, where they are reunited with the boy.

1 Arabesque

It was nearly a quarter-century after Alfred Hitchcock shot the
Marrakech sequences of *The Man Who Knew Too Much* (in the
spring of 1955) that the western world – perhaps Britain especially –
was stirred by Edward Said's pungent proclamation in *Orientalism*
that 'Asia speaks through and by virtue of the European imagination'
(p. 56). Said's Asia included the full range of exoticised non-
western civilisations, prototypically the Maghreb Arabs such as the
inhabitants of Morocco under French protection. Morocco is cited by
Said among a small group of Arab societies that have not 'developed
beyond dependence on the metropolitan West' (*Culture*, p. 252).
Nowadays, it has become fashionable to think of western
presentations of Arab culture – this Hitchcock film, as well as such
notable avatars as *The Barbarian* (1915), *The Sheik* (1924), and *The
Thief of Bagdad* (1940) – as deriving from 'European fear, if not
always respect' (*Orientalism*, p. 59), from dominating misperceptions
that colourised and spiced a relatively unknown cultural realm
through the agency of European – later American – imperatives,
initiatives, and prerogatives. But in 1956, for Hitchcock's audience
(his primary target), Morocco was a richer dream.

Western political machinations notwithstanding, Araby
remained in the imagination of Hollywood's audience a densely
embroidered vista of mysterious darkness, winding design, provocative
implication, unseen gesture, and alluring hints of romance. These
are the qualities that infuse the opening of *The Man Who Knew
Too Much*, with Hitchcock, his designer Henry Bumstead, and
his cinematographer Robert Burks deftly capturing the lambent
shock of Moroccan twilight, the confusion of untold masked bodies
shuffling under the stifling midday sun, and filigreed shadows of
exotic attraction and cloaked mystery – what Guy Davenport called
the arabesque, an 'intricate, nonrepresentational, infinitely graceful
decorative style' (p. 6). The soundtrack projects the muezzin's wail, a

marketplace storyteller's rhythmic barks, the tattoo of drums and rattle of tambourines. Here is a bold address to received understandings of the Arab world one could find illuminated in, for example, the *Tales of 1,000 Nights and One Night* (translated from the mid-nineteenth century), the fables of djinn and camel caravans, the luxe of Persian carpetry, the lush orchestrations of Rimsky-Korsakov's *Sheherezade*, the intoxicating story of Al-Ad'din and his magical incantation. Araby's sensuality overwhelms rationality, drowns calculation, defeats a commonplace, even stoutly liberalised western assertion of meaning.

Those who remember this film for its inclusion of Doris Day singing 'Que Sera, Sera' there may be stunned to learn that a full forty-five minutes are spent in Marrakech under the glare of the sun, under the whisper of the stars. The opening act is a dark labyrinthine vision. We begin with Dr Ben McKenna (James Stewart), his wife Josephine, formerly Jo Conway (Day), and their son Hank (Christopher Olsen) visiting the country in which Ben served during the war. On the Casablanca–Marrakech bus, they meet a stranger from France, Louis Bernard (Daniel Gélin),

The Marrakech daytime sequences were shot in 125°F temperatures, Hitchcock often working from inside an air-conditioned vehicle. Here, uncharacteristically, he has doffed his jacket. 'He was ready to go home as soon as he arrived' (Erickson to Brown)

who invites them to an exotic dinner but then inexplicably begs off (appearing with a date anyway, to Ben's infuriation).[1] In the restaurant, the McKennas meet and befriend a British couple, the Draytons (Bernard Miles, Brenda de Banzie), he involved with soil conservation research and she a staunch fan of 'the famous Jo Conway' (who had to give up her international singing career to become a housewife and mother). Next morning at the market, the two families witness a stabbing. The victim perishes in Ben's arms, but not before whispering that he is Bernard, and that an assassination is to take place soon in London. Summoned to make a witness statement at the Commissariat de police, the McKennas entrust Hank to Lucy Drayton's care.

During the police interrogation (civilised if imposing), Ben is called to the telephone, where an unidentified voice warns him that if he reveals a word of what Louis Bernard told him he will never see his son again. Hank, it seems, has been kidnapped and now, as we learn, both the child and the Draytons have disappeared.

A number of fascinating themes are woven through this section of the film:

Identity and masquerade

Identity is at best a puzzle, as is shown very early in the film. Bored young Hank, wandering up the aisle of the bus, stumbles when the driver swerves and catches her yashmak from a woman's face, openly revealing her for public recognition and appreciation, against strict religious dictate. The requirement of facial modesty was unknown at the time to Americans.[2] Irate, the woman's husband screams at the boy in hot-headed Maghreb Arabic, Ben rising swiftly, if without linguistic power, in his son's defence. It is at this point that Louis Bernard intercedes. He effectively calms the Arab, then explains to Ben that the Muslim religion 'allows for few accidents'. Consequently, teaches Bernard, 'There are moments in life when we all need a little help.' Instantly, a previously cached female face has been opened to sight; an apparently docile husband has morphed into an irrational and enraged accuser, calling Hank a *fialil kileb* (faithless

dog[3]); and the hitherto invisible Bernard is manifested as a skilful negotiator, a cultured traveller, and a curious and charming, if also inscrutable, new friend. All of this occurs in Hitchcock's elegant choreography within just a few minutes of screen time, *allegro*.

As our tourists descend from the bus in Marrakech's Place Djemaa el Fna ('Return of the Dead Souls'), Jo notices Bernard chatting sweetly with the outraged husband, as though long-time friends. She remarks on this to Ben, who mocks his 'famous' wife for being disgruntled to receive less attention than usual. She persists:

You don't know anything about this man, and he knows everything there is to know about you. ... He knows that ... that you live in Indianapolis, Indiana, he knows that you're a doctor at the Good Samaritan Hospital. And he knows that you attended a medical convention in Paris, and that you stopped off in Rome and Lisbon and Casablanca for just a few days ... And he knows that you, uh, served in North Africa in an Army field hospital.

The apparent openness of mutual introductions was a charade. For all his gracious help, Bernard is a man of mystery.

As the McKennas enter the Hôtel de la Mamounia from their *calèche*,[4] their paths are crossed by a well-dressed couple heading in the

Hitchcockian composition: note the triangle formed between the camera's (the viewer's) position and the lines of gaze of de Banzie and Day; and the second triangle involving the camera, Stewart's and Miles's head cant opposite direction. Jo is once again suspicious: they are being watched. A particularly elegant screen composition shows the two couples back to back, with the strange woman turning to catch a glimpse of Jo, and Jo turning to catch this glimpser glimpsing. Ben is still unconvinced, but in a subsequent shot, as the second couple settles into the carriage, it becomes clear that, yes, they have been looking at the McKennas, and with great curiosity. Facial and bodily gestures are quintessential in narrative film-making for conveying a character's alignment, intentionality, attitude, stance, and station, not to say feeling of the moment; here, however, we see in Hitchcock's brilliant (and strikingly economical) staging how gestures are also masks. Masks of intent or masks of camouflage?

Biography is another mask. Having been cordially invited by Bernard to 'a restaurant where the food is different and the manner of eating exotic', Ben and Jo are in their hotel room primping (Day in a spectacular $700 sleeveless green-print silk organdy dress with full skirt and wide shoulder straps, matching printed stole, and green leather contour belt [*Man Who Knew Too Much*, Production 1955–6 file][5]), with Jo seizing a moment to sing and dance with her son,[6] take delivery of his dinner from a waiter who has knocked at the door, and cut up his meat. (In the mid-1950s, a time when fast food was only newly born,[7] children were served adult-sized portions they could often not manage without a parent's intervention.) Bernard sips a cocktail with Jo on the balcony:

BERNARD   Were you on the American stage, Mrs McKenna?

JO   Yes, Mr Bernard, I was on the American stage. And the London stage and the Paris stage.

BERNARD   Oh?

JO   I thought perhaps you had seen me in Paris, being French.

BERNARD   Oh, you know, the theatre requires time, and for me time is often a luxury.[8]

JO   Have you ever been to Paris, Mr Bernard?

BERNARD   I was born there.

It is plain that Louis has discovered the depths of Jo's suspicion, her performative and motherly purpose. And that she will find out no more about him than he wants to reveal. What does he do for a living? 'I buy. And sell.' What? 'Whatever gives the most profit.' The cold politeness etched on Jo's face perfectly matches the elegant suaveness etched on his at this all-too-clear but all-too-uninformative display.

A sudden, second knock at the door.

A man (Reginald Nalder) standing in shadow is flooded by a wave of light. Slender, gracile, sharp-eyed, expensively dressed for the evening. 'Je m'excuse, mais je cherche la chambre de Monsieur Montgomery.' A voice quite unearthly in its musicality – the exact harmonic double of Jo's. Fluid, as though ariatic, enunciation. The lips and eyes gleaming shyly with politeness, except that the gaze passes Ben and Jo to pinpoint the figure at the back of the room. And, of course, the unforgettable face: not only gaunt, with cheekbones brazenly protruding, but with skin coarsely blemished from burns, warping the shape of a wise, perfectly girlish mouth.[9] Hitchcock, who in general disliked it, here uses the zoom to swoop into this face, so that the fine details of expression are rendered in portrait. The image is chilling but the sound of the voice is a lullaby: which is the mask? Within moments, Louis is speaking on the telephone in flustered French, and immediately thereafter he must cancel the dinner plans. He makes a courteous but speedy exit.

The restaurant is an undeclared triumph of Hollywood set design (and a virtuoso masking in itself). Henry Bumstead worked from photographs and detailed written descriptions of the Dar es-Salam, an actual restaurant in Marrakech visited for dinner by producer Herbert Coleman and unit production manager 'Doc' Erickson:

As we were about to dive into [the poulet au citron], the owner's French wife, in modern dress, came over to greet us and to remind us we must tear at the chicken only with the thumb and first two fingers of the right hand, messy but good. (Coleman to Hitchcock)

Bumstead had tiles hand-painted in Los Angeles, and fabrics imported (at $4 a yard, cheered Erickson). The long wall on the right banquette is 'wild' – that is, removable so that the camera can shoot the dinner party from that side. The screen 'reality' is thus, like so much in the story itself, utterly constructed.

Masks may fall away. Ben and Jo are seated, if, for him, with exceeding discomfort, on one of the too-plush banquettes. Another couple sits behind, and out of the corner of her eye Jo

Hitchcock's particular concern for the lighting effect on Nalder's face was articulated in an early storyboard drawing (well before casting)

Research photograph of the Dar es-Salam in Marrakech

Bumstead's $10,360 set on Paramount's Stage 1, where the restaurant sequence was shot between 27 and 29 June 1955 after ten days of construction

notices the woman stealing glances. But before Ben can disavow
her observations once more, the woman and her partner swivel
smilingly – the couple from outside the hotel! – and her voice chirps,
'You *are* the famous Jo Conway, aren't you?' So Jo's suspicion of
surveilling strangers was grounded: except with the wrong 'lighting'.
These are Lucy and Edward Drayton, two of her unknown and
valued fans, Edward a bit stodgy about 'this new be-bop' and Lucy as
gushingly friendly as any bucolic Englishwoman ever was. The four
join forces for an elaborate dinner of roast fowl, with Drayton
administering Ben a lesson (culled from Coleman's letter) on how to
use his fingers for eating. As Ben's ingenuous awkwardness takes centre
stage, the two women share entertained smiles. Abruptly, however,
Louis Bernard appears with his companion. Civil, jocular Ben flares
up, ready for confrontation, even a fist fight, over this snub. Under his
friendliness is a brittle sense of honour. Cut to a close shot of Bernard
and companion. *C'est ça la couple que tu cherches?* says she – 'That's
the couple you're looking for?' *Oui, c'est ça.* Bernard is a hunter.

For a supreme unmasking, the market chase:

'The chase seems to me the final expression of the motion
picture medium,' Hitchcock said in 1950 ('Core', p. 125).
A fugitive is fleeing a police squad through the busy alleys.
He charges into a dyer's vat of indigo, slips in the spill, and arises
covered in blue. Suddenly now, accompanied by the shrill police
whistles and crowd shouts,[10] he is pursued by a second figure in a
white djellaba, who catches up before the police do and plants a
dagger squarely in his back. The man staggers into the open, red
blood spotting his spine between two vertical lines of blue dye
(he is a red-blooded Blue Blood). Dark-skinned and stumbling in
Ben's direction, he kneels at the doctor's feet and slowly collapses,
his cheeks brushing the American's hands. In close shot, Ben
lifts his hands to see: brown make-up. This man is no Arab!
'Dr McKenna – I'm Louis Bernard,' the fatal whisper. So: a French
tourist and helper, a wise guide and philosopher, then a host and
subsequently non-host to an 'exotic' dinner, now a fleeing Arab,

now a dying white man. 'Poor fella,' Ben will recollect, with astounding correctness: a *fellah* in Arabic is a tiller of the soil. As *fellah*, Bernard cultivated a poor masquerade. Shortly afterwards, the Commissair de police (Yves Brainville) makes it plain that he was an agent of the Deuxième bureau.

Still more false identity, too close to home: Ben and Jo are with Edward Drayton at the commissariat, when in that interrupting phone call Ben learns his son is in danger. He quickly asks Drayton to phone the hotel and verify that Lucy and Hank got back all right. Drayton cannot raise the room, so Ben sends him off to find his wife and the child. When he and Jo show up soon afterwards, however, Ben learns that the Draytons have checked out. 'But he couldn't have! ... Mr Drayton, the Englishman, with the horn-rimmed glasses.' 'Yes, sir, he checked out.' Now a confrontation with Jo in their empty room is unavoidable. 'Something about this Louis Bernard and the police station and this whole spy business I haven't told you yet' – 'What?' The price of curiosity, says he, is that she take some sleeping pills. He is a doctor and he knows when and where to administer medication. Besides, 'You know what happens when you get excited and nervous ...' She baulks, but downs the pills so he will open up.

Bernard falling into Ben's arms, some of his 'Arab' swarthiness rubs off in the American's hands. This shot was made in 'reversal' at Gélin's suggestion, Stewart applying white make-up to Gélin's face (Personal correspondence)

'It wasn't any accident that Louis Bernard came up to us and helped us on the bus, started up a conversation. You were right about him. … He was on the lookout for a suspicious married couple':

JO   There's nothing very suspicious-looking about us, is there?
BEN   No … because he was wrong. It was a different married couple.
JO   Oh! And he was killed before he found them?
BEN   No. He found them. He found them, all right. It was in the restaurant where we had dinner last night, and that's one of the reasons he was killed.
JO   You'll be telling me next it's Mr and Mrs Drayton!
BEN   That's who it was, Jo.

But already, and swiftly, she is falling asleep. He tells her the Draytons have Hank. 'Hank!' – but the overpowering force of her maternity now thoroughly sedated, all she can do is scream shapelessly in anger. The Draytons, then, were not the harmless couple they pretended to be. Lucy's marketplace helpfulness – 'You don't want your little boy to go, do you?' – takes on a chilling second meaning. The woman's apparent generosity was a cold cunning.

Hitchcock's Araby, land of enchantments and entertainments – 'Marrakech: sounds like a drink!' Hank enthused on the bus – is a cavern of mirrors, a dark and twisting place in which treasure may be lost for ever.

Fatality
Behind the McKennas at the back of the bus as the story begins, and blatantly visible to us if not to them, is an 'ISSUE DE SECOURS' sign on the rear window: EMERGENCY EXIT. 'Get out now,' it proclaims, or, 'If you choose to remain, you will suffer the fate of the film.' Bernard's lesson about the Muslim religion allowing for 'few accidents' offers a clue that Ben and his family are in a territory

imbued with the belief in Fate. Here, events will overtake the agency of their wilful control.

A virtual anthem to fatality is Jo's bedtime song with Hank. Again and again we are treated to the simple, unforgettable refrain, 'Que sera, sera/Whatever will be, will be/The future's not ours to see/Que sera, sera/What will be, will be.' This conviction is an assertion of the complexity and indirectness of the world, man's humble, frail position in a far vaster scheme, and a paean to unseen forces, unworldly and unbounded, discerning and determining man's existence. Also sung is a relegation of quotidian concerns – 'What will I be?', 'What lies ahead?', 'What should I try?' – to the level of the very determinate; and, perhaps most pregnantly, a reflection of the power and operation of cinema itself, since for viewers, as for the characters, the cinematic future's 'not ours to see' until it presents itself onscreen in a continual and overwhelming unspooling that carries us along. 'That's the last time you're gonna hear *that* song,' Doris Day smirked, after finishing a recording session at Capitol Records under the direction of Frank DeVol (Livingston). But even there Fate took a hand, 'Que Sera, Sera' becoming a No. 1 pop hit and the song that iconised her future career.

Fatality lingers in the Arab restaurant, as the McKennas and Draytons collaborate to devour the roast squab they have ceremonially been served. After Drayton's pedantry about dining etiquette, we see arms extended toward the bird, hands stretching forth, fingers grasping at the tantalising flesh and then tearing the body asunder. The dramatic incoherence portrayed here – integration (of social form) becoming disintegration (of flesh) – is a testament to the place of (the bird's) powerlessness, incapacity, and ultimate passivity in the face of (human) dominating force. In a related way, the murder in the marketplace illustrates a fatalistic concurrence: the passive victim (Bernard) cannot run as fast as his murderer, who in a long passageway (and seen at first from above, so that the topology is plain) puts on a burst of speed,

catches up, and drives the dagger – an extension of the hand – when the poor *fella* is powerless to resist. The celebrated subsequent shot – where in medium focus (and accompanied by Bernard Herrmann's piercing brass chords) we see the as-yet-unidentified Bernard staggering away from the camera with those two blue lines of indigo dye framing the swelling red spot of blood – not only occupies, with perfect grammar, a position in the chain of moments that comprise the killing but also highlights the positioning of the wound outside the man's control. He in fact stretches his hand back to try for the knife handle and cannot find it.[11]

A notably alarming fatal moment occupies the centre of Ben's telephone conversation at the commissariat, in which he learns that Hank has been kidnapped. As we see him clutch the receiver to the side of his face, and hear the tinny distant voice at the other end, 'Dr McKenna? ...', Hitchcock performs what is for him a rather eccentric directorial gesture. We are carried in a jump-cut to a high shot of a discontiguous room in which this call has originated. From behind, we see a man seated in a large chair, a delicately tiled floor spreading away at his feet. Listening to his threatening voice, we watch in suspension, the elegantly composed room a crypt of silence, the identity of the persona unrevealed.

Shot on location in Marrakech, a 'poor *fella*' staggers toward death with indigo drying on his back

This is a single shot, unrepeated in the film (and as a grammatical statement, unrepeated in Hitchcock's oeuvre). Another film-maker would have stayed on Ben's reacting face and let the soundtrack carry the message, but we are given a view of the remote spirit directing and arranging events: a view, too, from a calculating but unknowing gaze.

The man looking for Monsieur Montgomery in the Mamounia doorway is another fascinating cipher of fatality. His brutally scarred face and gauntness instantly convey mystery and chilling threat, while his gracious etiquette and sophistication of language, the precision of his Parisian accent, his controlled breathing, and his elegant posture all intimate sociability, charm, breeding, and propriety – a division accented by the flash lighting and zoom. With this figure – as with the population in the Djemaa el Fna, living and pulsing yet covered from head to toe in soft flowing robes – there is a split between the unseen inner world of sensation, feeling, drive, and desire and the visible outer shell of circumstance, performance, and grooming. The impossibility of penetrating from appearance to spirit is confounding, rendering one passive to the breath of Fate.

Remote force

A hidden object

The Hitchcockian view of Marrakech swirls relentlessly in a search for the unlocatable. A vortical, non-directional view of the market with the multidimensional throng and their passions; the fugitive's flight from the police (and his inability to flee from Death) in twisting, seemingly dislocated byways; the turning of the McKenna–Bernard relationship through various familiarities toward strangeness; the constant flow of voices and fugitive visions. In this complex and indeterminate Islamic world, a hallowed object is lost, evanesces: the spirit, the innocent, the untouched. Note a precursor: the bus, site of Hank's jarring discomfiture and first focus of our attention, dissolves in the crowd as it crawls into the city. Note how the Arab wife's veil, apparent point of dispute, evaporates and is forgotten. Or how the penetrating gaze of strangers, initially Jo's point of focus, dissipates through their self-identification and familiarity. Or how the food in the restaurant, Ben's plague and Jo's delight, is backgrounded through the exacting difficulties of table manners. Or how the beautiful twilight outside the McKenna hotel suite, solid as a jewel, becomes an enticing, confounding atmosphere of doubt, possibility, and phantom presence.

But for Jo, one object shines as central proposition: the body and character of Hank. Doted upon, played with, shepherded with care, then suddenly made to disappear like a magician's assistant. He is constructed for brightness (intellectual and optical), thus as a treasure token. It is Hank who through his childish clumsiness precipitates the engagement of Louis Bernard with the McKennas on the bus, this ultimately leading the Frenchman to find Ben 'out of five thousand people, in a great marketplace' to hear his dying confession. It is Hank who introduces us to the singing and dancing body, reprised by the natives in the market who represent what D. H. Lawrence might call the 'spirit of place'. It is Hank who is first caught by the flamboyance of the chase, whose initial attempts to run off in the direction of the fugitive, curtailed helpfully by Lucy Drayton, lead the camera to follow, thus paving the way toward the grave denouement of Bernard's death.

And it is bright Hank's double – 'Hank' the missing cipher – who bounds and establishes Ben and Jo's commitment and forward movement. As the missing object in a city throbbing with movement and chaos, the child comes perfectly to symbolise the riddle and challenge, the narrative purpose, and the philosophical reason of the entire film: life as a search through time for what is finally elusive. At a poignant moment in the shadows of night, with Jo but half-awake on her bed of grief, Ben silently packs their bags – folding away the tiny sports coat – and comes upon Hank's baseball mitt. This pathetic little thing, coming suddenly from out of the blue, instantly metonymises the absent boy and stands in for absence itself. It is America, American consciousness, and American strangeness in Africa, the baseball mitt a cherished treasure but only if the little boy who awarded it his love ever touches it again, or we set eyes upon him. Lost, lost, irretrievably lost is Hank now, in all this traffic of souls, through all the myriad voices, with the stars above the turquoise firmament signalling nothing, and all the world covering his trace. Should Ben and Jo wait in Marrakech for a signal, since Hank's voice, now shrunk in the multitude, may at any moment cry out? Or should they follow the Draytons to England, hoping against hope, and fearing at every breath that they may have left the reason of their lives behind?

2 Wild-Goose Chase

Hitchcock arranges for Louis Bernard's dying secret to be confided in an astonishing shot – especially for 1956 viewers lucky enough to see the original Technicolor prints projected in their VistaVision format upon a very large screen.[1] Bernard has collapsed to the ground, his arm caught around Ben's neck to draw the doctor's ear close. We are watching from beneath and behind the dying man, peering up at Ben's slow comprehension as we hear the words fading off in whispers. 'A man, a statesman, is to be killed, assassinated, in London. Soon, very soon. Tell them in London, "Ambrose Chappell".' The famous Jimmy-Stewart face is shot in macro-close-up, so that it fills the entire screen from top to bottom, blue eyes darting left and right to accompany Bernard's stilted breathing; lips slightly parted; the expression a quintessential model of attentiveness. London, evidently, is the next port of call.

Even as the McKennas' plane taxis into London Airport (latterly London Heathrow), we can note a shift in the palette from a gilded, turquoise-accented sunny glare to a restrained, blue-tinted overcast haze. Stiffness and seriousness present themselves on all fronts in London Town, especially in a private interview with

Paramount's VistaVision used a 1.85:1 ratio. In many theatres, this shot would appear, stunningly, on a screen fifty or more feet wide

Buchanan (Ralph Truman) of Scotland Yard's Special Branch,
where Ben and Jo are implored, even threatened, to share what they
heard from Bernard (dispatched to Morocco at the Yard's request).
For Hank's safety, Ben adamantly refuses.

A plush hotel room at the Savoy. Ben is searching the phone
directory for Ambrose Chappell. He locates an address in Camden
Town and makes an appointment, but the man turns out to be
completely innocent. Back at the hotel, however, Jo realises it's a
church, not a man! Returning to the directory, she discovers an address
for Ambrose Chapel in Bayswater and heads off there. As she lingers
outside, we enter to discover Lucy Drayton adjusting the hymn board
then mounting to an upper study where her husband, now in clerical
garb, is briefing an assassin to make his shot at a precise downbeat
in the finale of a choral work to be performed at a concert that night.
The killer is none other than the gaunt visitor from the hotel corridor
in Marrakech. Lucy retires to an adjacent room where Hank is placidly
defeating his minder at checkers. Ben now joins Jo in the street outside
and in tandem they enter the chapel while a service is in progress.

Spying the McKennas, Lucy signals her husband at his
podium and Ben sends Jo off to ring Buchanan. Drayton breaks
off his sermon, sending the congregation home and locking Ben in.

'It's not a man, it's a place!'

Ben screams out for Hank, and hearing the boy's distant response tries to rush upstairs but is coshed by a henchman. In a call box, Jo reaches Buchanan's assistant, Woburn (Noel Willman), who promises to fetch the police, while in a rear view of the chapel we watch the boy and the Draytons being chauffeured away. Ambrose Chapel is quiet as a grave when the police finally arrive. They persuade Jo to take a ride in the direction of the Albert Hall, where she may find Buchanan. Meanwhile, Ben awakes from his stupor, climbs the bell rope, and perches in the belfry[2] as the ringing attracts the attention of local residents.

At the Albert Hall, Jo has eyes peeled for Buchanan. She catches him entering in a parade of dignitaries, but is swiftly confronted by the Assassin, who, with a familiar, cordial smile, warns, 'You have a very beautiful little boy, Madame. His safety will depend upon you tonight,' before marching upstairs to his box (the box *we* know he will use as a shooting platform). The concert begins. With its

Bumstead's Chapel set on Stage 5 at Paramount. Shooting took place on 8 and 9 July 1955 (with the hymn directly recorded on the 9th); 11–12 (with direct recording both days); 18–19 (with playback of the recording)

two movements, 'Storm Clouds' mirrors the film's division so far: an opening *Lento* echoing the meditative, querulous, almost mystic setting in Marrakech that causes Jo (at the back of the auditorium) to swoon with fear and musical sensitivity, and cues the Assassin, at its conclusion, to begin his preparation; and an *Allegro agitato*, when Ben arrives, Jo 'tells' him what she thinks is happening, and he, 'getting the picture', races upstairs to urge the police into action. The stalwart London bobbies of course pay him no heed. He must dash from box to box, hoping to find the right one before it is too late. Downstairs, Jo is at the end of her tether as the music mounts inexorably to its climax, and in the final moment, when the cymbalist is to bring his cymbals together, she screams. 'Everybody has the same feeling why I screamed in that movie and they know why I did. It's just elementary,' I was told by Day. (Yet legion are the viewers convinced Jo screams to foil the assassination, a complete

Bumstead's set for the Chapel rear on Paramount's transparency Stage 2. This became part of a rear-projection composite, with the camera high on a crane and the action of Jo pacing the street on the other side projected in

impossibility, because unlike us she was not cued.) The shooter's aim is fractured, Ben bursts into the box and forces him onto the railing (for a moment, graceful as a dancer), whence he plummets to his death in the seats below. Now the house manager (Richard Wattis) insists on escorting Jo across the lobby so that she can be introduced to the foreign Prime Minister (Alexei Bobrinskoy), whose life she has saved, and his blushing Ambassador (Mogens Wieth). From this gesture will assuredly flow Hank's recovery, and the reuniting of the McKenna family.

While the chase in the Marrakech marketplace was enacted briskly, to the charge of rattling drums, the extended hunt for Hank through London is more prolonged, equivocal, and troubling. Seeking a figure who could be anywhere, Ben and Jo are forced to rush 'toward' him with no topography in mind, from Camden Town to Bayswater, from the Strand to Kensington and Mayfair. It is urgent they find their hidden object (just as it is urgent the Cantata 'find' its 'release'), but the hunt is excruciatingly optical and circumstances have made them blind. To make matters even worse for Ben and Jo, yet more entertaining for viewers, Hitchcock provides an obstacle course:

The scream that does not directly cause a missing boy to materialise. According to the rules of the plot, which Jo knows as well as we do, she may well be helplessly condemning Hank at this instant

Distant voices

A contrast to the softly lit police office in Marrakech, where the chief inspector sat puffing on a pipe and everyday sounds wafted through his window,[3] the sordid little room confronting Ben and Jo as soon as they disembark in London seems a chilly, unforgiving bureaucratic cell. Buchanan is all postures: etiquette, composure, seriousness, cool grace. About the prize he covets he is unrelentingly pressing. Yet nothing will squeeze Bernard's secret from Ben, even applying emotional pressure to Jo's already severely frayed nerves. The situation darkens measurably with a ring of the telephone. Here again, as with the terrifying caller in Marrakech earlier, Hitchcock employs an extreme Dutch angle, shooting down upon Ben and Jo as they clutch at the receiver as though it were a life raft. Lucy Drayton's familiar chirrup, and Hank's, are recorded in such a way that 'coming through the wire' they seem reduced, as though projected from an indeterminate distance, and distinctly metallic. Biological they may be, but one senses links to the mechanism of the phone system. With their mechanical voices, Lucy and Hank might

Nalder with Hitchcock during one of the Albert Hall lobby set-ups. 'Somebody brought him in,' Herbert Coleman told me, 'and Hitch's face changed. He said, "All you have to have is one glance at this man." They decided instantaneously' (Personal correspondence)

be automatons, while Ben and Jo, anxious, frantic, and fully present in the flesh, are magnified in organic feeling by comparison. By an internal logic of cinema, the further away Hank seems, the more unlikely the promise of finding him.

Buchanan appears a pleasant enough man to whom one could feel comfortable turning for help, except that he is plainly groping in the dark with no help to give. Overhead are heard myriad take-offs and landings, brutal reminders that an army of untold eager strangers is shuttling here to zealously cover the world. Once again: an incalculably large field in which to find a tiny soul.

Uninvited guests

A paralysing distraction:

Wary and demoralised, Ben and Jo enter their Savoy suite in need of warmth, privacy, and ease, if only momentary. The plush furnishings, mahogany tables, and beautiful appointments all presage comfort, but prominent bouquets from show business chums proclaim unseen pals 'waiting in the wings', ready, one might fear, to convert Hank's absence from a trauma into a secret (the film's second principal such item, a match for Bernard's dying confidence) by constituting an audience for a family performance. We are placed by Hitchcock's

A voice coming from a long way off

narrative architecture on a cusp between two urgent concerns: to penetrate Bernard's secret and assist in protecting the 'statesman' who is 'to be killed'; and to guard the McKennas' secret and keep Val and friends from learning what Ben and Jo don't want known, that Hank has been taken from their hands. As these two secrets are bound together, Ben and Jo's silence constituting the guarantee of Hank's safety, the conundrum seems unresolvable. The twinned

Ease of telecommunication in tonal darkness. A curious graphic clarity binds two desperate moments, planned in advance in storyboard sketches: London Airport; telephone booth near Ambrose Chapel

telephone calls, one in Marrakech and one in London, state the terms of this dilemma acoustically as well as dialogically: the unidentified or unlocatable voice sounding in a cocoon of darkness. Ben is just concluding arrangements with Ambrose Chappell (Ambrose: fourth-century resolver of conflict and patron of the poor[4]), when a third knock comes upon a door, Fate's signal – privacy and rest seem entirely elusive in Hitchcockian hotels, which cater, like airports, to interminably migrating strangers on the move. Where, we could wonder, in all this shuffling and criss-crossing of personae, is the home of the spirit (a question Hitchcock would have his villain Adamson raise explicitly in *Family Plot* [1976])? When Jo opens the door, in burst:

Val Parnell (Alan Mowbray), his wife Helen (Alix Talton), Cindy Fontaine, formerly Elva MacDuff 'from Harrisburg P-A' (Carolyn Jones), and the air-headed but oh-so-chic Jan Peterson (Hillary Brooke), a blithe quartet dressed for court and gushing with eagerness to see Jo again: see her and meet the oh-so-talked-about good Doctor. But where is the little boy?, the chums beg to know. 'He's staying with some other people so we could have a little time by ourselves,' comes an equivocal answer, efficient, uninformative, as Ben makes excuses, begging Val to handle the drinks, and rushes off. Val, with a disappointed probe: 'I'd like to see which one of you he looks like.'

Desperate to join Ben, Jo is now trapped by the strictures of etiquette as a virtual prisoner to camaraderie, the London gang pattering on about showbiz nonsense of no concern to her frazzled maternal self. Yet she is doubly caught. If hunger for reuniting her family eats at her, the courtesy afforded to Val Parnell by 'the famous Jo Conway' reflects that he was one of the primary producers of her fame. The filmic 'Val Parnell' was, indeed, Val Parnell (his name used with permission), one of the leading lights in British theatrical production of the 1940s. If Jo is to have any hope of a future at the Palladium, Val is her ticket. Hitchcock's attentiveness to so picayune an item of dramaturgy merits notice: he uses a character like Parnell rather than any conveniently made-up manikin who could have undertaken the same dramatic action. After they have been waiting some time for Ben to return, the puissant Val it is who, even here and now, opens a golden door – if quite inadvertently: 'Jo, what's become of that unpredictable husband of yours? He's been gone over an hour now. He went to see some man, what was it? Church?' At which point, hearing his words echo, she stands from her chair in shock at the realisation that 'It's not a man, it's a place!' The thought of there being more potential, more underpinning, in a place than a person makes for a special frisson.

Friendly intrusion seemed to place social burdens on Jo and Ben for which they had neither patience nor resources. But these four charming apparent barriers to the McKennas' higher purpose (of which no clue can be offered) are angels of mercy in disguise.

Animalia

Ben's escapade in meeting Ambrose Chappell forms a complex little play-within-the-play. As he strides quietly up Pearman Street from Westminster Bridge Road, he hears his footsteps echoing against the long line of town houses. But when he pauses and the echo persists, he knows with a chill that someone else is there – initially a ghost, then presently a tall cipher bearing a trenchcoat. Ben continues apace, with some trepidation, as the figure gains on him and moves forward to the corner. Tousled hair, steady, even dreamy gaze studying the entrance to the little mews Ben must take to find: AMBROSE CHAPPELL TAXIDERMIST. This is where the man heads, too, passing Ben at the corner, leading the way onward, yet glancing back over his shoulder to see who is following him. Ben follows, and as he enters the vacant, aged, narrow bricked passageway, the camera simulates his progress toward the green door that protects Chappell's premises. The shop set, Henry Bumstead confided to me, was inspired by an actual, hundred-year-old taxidermy shop that had been operated for generations by the Gerrard family (Personal conversation). Inside the green-painted, densely compacted warren of stuffed lions, cats, swordfish, birds, and other animals, Ben finds: not one but two

Ambrose Chappells, father and son (the man from the sidewalk), who have no knowledge whatever of a child, a kidnapping, or any such nefarious business but who ring the police when Ben implies they must be covering something up. To escape their 'jungle', Ben is forced to struggle through the staff shuffling around the room bearing creatures like cherished infants, and as the scene concludes he finds himself poised with a hand inside a great cat's maw. Ambrose Chappell is a dead end, as the mews structure hinted. What deeper purpose might underpin Hitchcock's funny, somewhat alien scene?

First, to reiterate the recurring theme of doubling: two cities, two police inspectors, two hunts, plenty of double identities. Now: footsteps and echoes; older and younger taxidermists; Ben's intense conviction of their connection to the missing Hank coupled with the Chappells' entire lack of knowledge. Also doubled are all the beasts in the shop, each stuffed effigy a second version of the same creature in life, a stilled image to stand in for the absent breathing one. In the same way, the film offers us effigies in place of lives, yet effigies that we take to be satisfying and revealing. The missing Hank alive in Ben's mind is an effigy, too, a phantom.

Ambrose Chappell's, built in London for shooting (2–4 June 1955). Richard Wordsworth (left) and George Howe with Stewart. 'I remember looking at the shop and it was tiny,' Bumstead told me. 'I built an office and everything'

The taxidermy shop also openly and blatantly introduces animality, returning us to the brutality of the marketplace stabbing and the seductive tactility of the Marrakech environment with its energised dancers and 'exotic' meal, and offers a stunning contrast to the tautly spatialised, socialised labour on evidence during the Cantata performance where the surge of feelingful expression is shaped, disciplined, and controlled. The chaos at Ambrose Chappell's recalls the vicious emotionalism of the bus argument, and the stifling

Note the hand work. Top: Barbara Howitt, with Bernard Herrmann on the podium

etiquette imposed in both the conversation with Buchanan and the guests' arrival at the Savoy. Ben and the two Ambroses begin relating through rational, conventional strategies that civilly guide and shape their interaction, but soon emotions have taken over and bodies, rough gestures, gesticulations, and collisions have replaced orderly discourse. In this melee, Ben is relatively passive, confirmed as a man of intellect and order with a clear idea of how things ought to be if not exactly how things are. The animals, by contrast, do not *know* at all, they sense. Or at least they sensed while they lived, at this point *representing sense* instead. Counterposed against human movement or ferried around the room for safety, they appear to live again: as the chorus will intone in the Cantata, 'Panic overtook each flying creature of the wild.'

The preservation of animals through taxidermy is a form of spirit worship related to primitive *intichiuma*, central in totemism (Frazer, p. 130). The stuffed animal is a puzzle, since the configuration of muscles and hairs constituting its expressive demonstration is produced through artful human intervention after death, not intrinsic spirit and intelligence during life. Taxidermy is a post-mortem taming,

'Panic overtook each flying creature of the wild'

a special case of animal domestication. The 'game' of taxidermy[5] can use an unthreatening beast as a stage for recreating a masque of danger, the sort of masque played out by Ben in the restaurant, with his table companions' support, where hunger and incapacity continually invoke danger (Ben falls over trying to tear meat from the bone). And, what Ben McKenna did to his squab Ambrose Chappell's lion soon later 'threatens' to do to him. That lion, framed to remove evidence of its pose in a shop, appears to contemplate leaping at McKenna, eyes focused, jaws opened in savagery. The taxidermist's assistants hold Ben by the arms as though to position him for sacrifice. Thus is he seemingly 'fed to the lions', a reincarnation of faithful Daniel or of the Christians in the Coliseum who reincarnated him. Seeing taxidermy, we survey the panorama of nature, sense the heights that human arrangements have gained. With inherent contradiction, what the 'creature' is apparently 'doing' and what the thing ostensibly 'is' do not match.

'Uncivilised' reality is 'taxidermically' altered in our imagination. Consider in this light the great cat's tooth-baring growl. Baring its teeth, the beast is read as 'hungry', ready to pounce. But in nature, hungry lions do not predictably display a signal mask 'readable' to the prey. For lions, the grimace may be no sign at all, while for humans, who make signs and live by them, it is. The meaningful 'hunger' of the lion in the taxidermy shop is thus entirely Ben's – and our – construction, as are all the bestial expressions there. In pretending the lion 'wishes' to 'dine upon' Ben, we project onto it – an easy mark – elements of our own motivation. We gaze at our own sign system, but as etched upon the face of a lion not a person. In the projection, we forget ourselves projecting, focus exclusively on the beastly face. This anthropomorphosis allows us an extraordinary vantage: not only is the animal like us in signing as we would; we are like him. The taxidermy shop allows us to see how beastly we are.

A sad chapel

Their pathway straightened as well as straitened, Ben and Jo arrive in the bleak little non-denominational chapel where Drayton is intoning to his congregation that they should 'take stock' of their lives (as his assistant Edna[6] pounds away on the organ and docile Lucy traipses up the aisle taking collection). The congregation is wailing a hymn from the Magdalen Chapel called 'The Portents',[7] with some few alterations of wording effected at the hand of Bernard Herrmann: 'Wherefore do earthquakes cleave the ground/Why hides the sun in shame?' The feeling here is one not of spiritual uplift but of worldly depression and resignation, indeed shame, as though the hard realities of class distinction and deprivation in London's long and vitiating postwar austerity (clearly exemplified in this congregation) trump any hope of either religious fervour or genuine pride (on postwar British class issues, see Kynaston, *Austerity*). Class consciousness was always important in Britain, and signally important to Hitchcock.

Is Edward Drayton the orator a genuine man of the cloth, somehow perverted by the thirst for power and sucked into a brutal assassination plot which does not command the deep faith of his heart? Or, as the Assassin archly suggests, is he in truth only a low thug, posing as a middle-class minister? In the rehearsal scene, the Assassin had class-consciously mocked him – 'a wolf in sheep's clothing': viciousness garbed as innocence but also abasedness pretending to power. Drayton is certainly the weekly figure on this

Drayton teaching table manners

dais, the man his congregants recognise as their normal sermoniser, but does that discount the possibility of him harboring evil? We note of Drayton that he wears clerical garb only for leading his service, and that his vocal pattern when he speaks of adversity is markedly performative. Reading from the man to the place, we must ask, is this hollow shell his 'sheep's clothing' – his sheepskin! – or is it his genuine home? There is something depressive in Drayton, too, a tone of abject surrender. He is more desperate than his wife, less at home in this bleak space. The Ambrose Chapel is *unheimlich*. Ben and Jo only sham a homely attitude there: singing along with the congregation, her voice is too strong, too professional; and he uses the melody to conceal a lyric of his own devising, 'Ahh–ahhh, this-is-jusssst another willd–goooose–chaaaaase.'

As to the wild-goose chase: 'Thou has more of the wild-goose in one of/thy wits than, I am sure, I have in my whole five,' proclaims Mercutio in *Romeo and Juliet* (Act 2 Scene 4), lending sufficient definition to reveal how incandescent little Hank could be something of a 'wild goose' for his admiring father. For all its glamour, London is indeed a wild-goose chase for the McKennas, and Drayton's words of consolation to his weepy congregation apply as well to Ben and Jo, perforce listening in: 'The average life, yours and mine,

Preaching on adversity

is often harassed and perplexed, by disappointment and by cruelties beyond our control. Now, strangely enough, it is often these things beyond our control which help.' In the wild-goose chase, what seem like obstructions may not really be obstructions at all. What appears to misdirect us lights the way. A Scotland Yard inspector musing, 'A good agent keeps on staking his life. He doesn't always win.' An unexpected guest announcing, 'When your mind gets sick of your body, it does something to it.' An old taxidermist reflecting, 'I think I understand your problem. You expected someone else.' A false minister, aficionado of symphonic music, preaching, 'Few of us pause to consider how life's adversities work in our behalf to make better men and women of us. But I think we should pause, and pause now, ... to look into our own hearts and lives and see what we find there.'[8] Each one of these Stations of the Cross contains a secret message that Ben and Jo might hear and take to heart in their search: Ben more than Jo, indeed, because, surely, he is the man who (always already) knows too much – not in the sense that in his mental stores the shelves contain too much information (because often information is missing for him) but in that as contingencies arise, he makes *knowing* his method of choice. When in doubt, he opines and investigates.

But investigation is a gamble. Thought and embodiment live separate lives. Our understandings are fragile, beware of trusting them. Only through suffering will come salvation.

3 I Heard Voices

Ray Evans and Jay Livingston's 'Que Sera, Sera' was not written with Doris Day in mind.[1] They got word that Hitchcock was looking for a popular song (they shared Lew Wasserman with him as agent) and went up to Louis Lipstone's office to play it for him on the piano. 'I don't know what kind of a song I want,' said Hitchcock, 'but that's *it*.' He also took their 'We'll Love Again', the lyrical ballad that Jo sings to entertain the Prime Minister and his guests at the embassy: 'Now it's goodbye/And we're facing such lonely tomorrows!'[2] While his music director, Bernard Herrmann, was outspoken in his revulsion for 'Que Sera' – 'What do you want a piece of crap like that in the movie for?' (Livingston) – Hitchcock's creative impulse was arrow true, 'Que Sera, Sera' (and 'Love Again', as well) perfectly showcasing Jo's vocative power; emblematising the saccharine but evocative fare she would have used for building an international career; and bringing lyricism to the emotional turn of the film. The voice is central in *The Man Who Knew Too Much*.

Jo enjoys international popularity as a paragon of vocal expression. Her husband points to her fame obliquely on the way to the Mamounia, when she tries to persuade him that because he asked Ben a lot of questions but revealed nothing about himself 'Mr Bernard is a very mysterious man.' His playful rejoinder, 'You're sore because he didn't ask *you* any questions,' addresses a *you* targeted by reporters around the world: *you*, accustomed to being queried about your professional and personal life; *you*, perennial centre of attention. 'Hardy har har,' retorts she.[3] On the hotel balcony with Bernard, Jo is explicit about her stage experience. And at the restaurant, her discovery that the woman who has been eyeing her is one of her many fans – 'You *are* Jo Conway? The famous Jo Conway?' – makes her oblivious to Lucy's disingenuousness. At the embassy, after the Albert Hall debacle, the Prime Minister graciously takes her hand: 'I hear you are *the famous* Jo Conway, Madame.' And his Ambassador

Christopher Olsen singing 'Que Sera, Sera' with Doris Day; Olsen rehearsing the dance moves on set with choreographer Nick Castle

happily informs the (tedious) assembly of dignitaries: '*The famous* Jo Conway has gladly consented to sing a few songs for us tonight.' Reprising the theme of the singer's fame is her voice heard at the top of the embassy where Hank is hidden. It sounds like a phonograph recording of itself, distantly removed from, and through mass circulation elevated above, the pulse of live presence.

As played by the famous Doris Day, 'the famous Jo Conway' is nothing if not a model of performative sensitivities. Keenly observant, artfully calculating, but at the same time a fount of melodious sentiment and a master at phrasing, she embodies the vocality she effortlessly puts on display. Jo is never at a loss for words or expressive gesture, while her husband bumbles his way through the narrative from one inarticulate, grasping moment to another – 'Wait just a minute ...', 'Wait a minute, hold on here ...' – cudgelling others to align their actions and thoughts with his less flexible ones. Ben also cherishes received ideas about the world in which he moves: that pictures are faithful renditions of reality; that the thronged marketplace is full of business and passion, not secrets; that Louis Bernard's amicability displays true friendship (thus Ben's ire at being stood up in the restaurant); that the man at the hotel room door really was searching for Monsieur Montgomery; that the Draytons actually are the charming innocents they seem. Jo's responses to situational contingencies are felt and expressive, even contradictory – she yearns for another child but also for continuance of her singing career in New York – while Ben's are rational and down to earth, which is to say, grounded (uncharged). He understands the likes of Alida Markle's asthma, Herbie Taylor's ulcers, and Mrs Yarrow's potential triplets, but not melodies. Thus Ben interprets Bernard's secret message in a literal, pedestrian way: to him, 'Tell them in London, "Ambrose Chappell"' means: locate a particular person, make a deal. It is Jo who, with Val Parnell's help, *hears* rather than *reads* the secret message: for her, 'Ambrose Chapel' is sonic not iconic. She is consistently one who acts upon taste, sentiment, sensation, and the rhythm of experience. Indeed, her emotionalism

transcends the everyday and enters the domain of the operatic, as we easily see in the Albert Hall by her anxious response to the ongoing fact of Hank's absence, to the violence she suspects and fears, and also to the glory of Arthur Benjamin's choral music.

During the Cantata, Hitchcock builds a fascinating triangle. Jo is at the back of the hall, a quintessential listener, with harmony and poetry unfurling from the stage before her as she rhapsodises in her expensive dove-grey Italian silk suit, from which light shimmers as she turns or positions her hands. The official performer of the moment, Barbara Howitt, is in radiant cobalt blue upon a stage lined with pink blossoms, singing lyrics as if she believed them. And the tuxedoed Assassin, attentive to every nuance of the music, sports opera glasses and opened ears. The Assassin is listening as intently as Jo, concentrating on the lifting and dropping phrases as fully as the singer (we see him peeking at his partner's pocket score). Like Howitt, Jo needs no score: to her the music makes sense intrinsically, because more than a mother, wife, tourist, or searcher, she is a singer, too, whose every hearing breath imitates the phrasing onstage. When the singer and chorus chant about 'flying creatures of the wild', Jo intuits that

Lucy seeing Jo; the Assassin seeing the Prime Minister (Nalder wore his own tuxedo)

they are referencing life itself, the film viewers, the concert audience with their manifold currents of feeling and desire. 'Yet stood the trees/ Around whose head screaming/The night birds wheeled/and shot away.' The Cantata is a fauvist scape, mystical, ethereal, invoking the flow of blood, hesitation, want, absence, memory, and movement, to all of which Jo responds hyper-rationally. Ben racing through the corridors to find the shooter is a paragon of rationality. But Jo's scream is purely musical and purely emotive, a 'note' inscribed in Hitchcock's composition.

The magnitude of Jo's expressiveness – a characterisational requirement so long as we are to consider her a realistic portrait of internationally celebrated pop-musical fame – helps explain a passage in the film that viewers unresponsive to Day's careful performance may find problematic – the medication scene at the Mamounia. Ben administers a tranquilliser – 'I make my living knowing how and when to administer medicine' – as a prelude to revealing that the Draytons absconded with Hank. By the time his words click, Jo is sufficiently sedated to be incapable of a full response, and explodes at having been controlled this way. To understand this quintessentially Hitchcockian moment as more than a controlling put-down of the principal female character, we must look at the architecture that supports it. Dramatically, Ben's medicating his wife stands upon two important infradiegetic realities. First, having forsaken a singing career for motherhood, Jo has made Hank the centre of her life (for better or worse): this centre has forcefully been removed, and the boy may well die. She is overwhelmed by shocking impotence and surrounded, at least as she must feel it, by a ring of impenetrable darkness. Surely echoing for her, as for us, at this moment is Hank's distant, tinny voice on Buchanan's phone, his being at one time *here* and *not here* in the most exacting way.

Much worse, however – even unbearable for Jo – is what she must instantly remember on hearing that, of all people, it is Lucy Drayton who has taken Hank away: *she herself gave the boy to his kidnapper,* openly, forthrightly, and in total ignorance of a reality she failed to perceive:

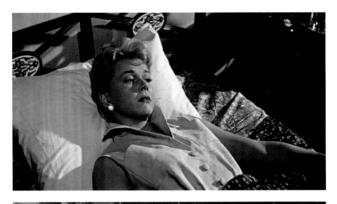

Lost, lost, irretrievably lost; making the Mamounia bedroom shot

LUCY   I think it better if I take him back to the hotel, don't you?

JO   Would you please?

That the deeper reality was invisible at the time, beyond her powers, is immaterial against the blunt fact of the boy's absence and her guilt. At once, then, Jo is immeasurably despondent and at sea. An authentic reaction from her would be strong, uncontainable, and possibly self-damaging. Perhaps Ben *does* know when to administer medication, and this *is* the time.

But Ben McKenna aside, Hitchcock has quite another problem, bearing upon the structure of his film as a whole. If Jo should react with intemperate honesty to her son's kidnapping,[4] her expressiveness would needs hit a register entirely off-key with all the tonality of the film so far, not just extreme but unmeasurable. More problematic still: a moment planned for a vital turning point later, the climactic scream at the Royal Albert Hall, would become a mere echo if Jo released herself fully now. Some dramaturgical mechanism was needed in the hotel room to hold her response down while at the same time permitting its authenticity. Jo's drugged collapse is thus preparation for her explosion during the Cantata.

But the turnings and echoes of the film's musicality are more complex still:

Lucy offering to babysit. Note de Banzie's telltale performative gesture, the tight right-handed grasp of Olsen's shoulder, and Day and Stewart's entire failure to focus upon it

Orchestration

The story begins on the way to Marrakech, but the film, a continuing counterplay of sight against sound, does not. When the VistaVision logo disappears, we are confronted with a sight that blares musicality, an orchestra performing onstage in the great cavern of the Royal Albert Hall. Call this an overture. As the credits appear, the camera glides in for a progressively closer view of the players until finally we rest upon the cymbalist. Lifting his twin shining brass concavities beside his head, he becomes a personage with monstrous ears. The clue: pay special heed to sound and its role, sound notably musical and carefully orchestrated. Sound is memory, the past, rhythm, hope, and harmony, as well as recognisable timbre (the motherly or any other voice). Sound is connection: 'In general, what we see of a man will be interpreted by what we hear from him' (Simmel, p. 357). Also distinct in the opening shot is a microcosm of the organised social world, the order that will see disruption as the film proceeds.

As a panoply of cooperative workers, the orchestra models Émile Durkheim's 'organic solidarity', an emblem especially of modern life: many disparate operators act to achieve different aspects of an accomplishment, which comes into existence because

Hearing and instrumentation

of the interrelated organisation of parts. Durkheim's contrasting 'mechanical solidarity' will be manifested in the choir, as dozens upon dozens of singers with the same vocal range – sopranos, altos, tenors, basses – are massed together to produce action in magnified force (the magnification audible and visible against the soloist who stands in front). The orchestral organicism reflects upon that of the film production itself (where actors and technicians work independently but toward a collaborative goal); as well as that of the story, especially the working of its plot through a weaving of personalities, places, and moments: that, labouring under the direction of unseen forces and for ends we must wait to learn, agents have imported to England a man whose well-disciplined actions can be aligned with, of all things, a musical score. This assassin will become, in effigy, a member of the orchestra, taking his cue from the conductor's downbeat. During the secret rehearsal, Drayton smugly described the culminating musical moment: 'Even the listeners will be undisturbed. I think the composer would have appreciated that, don't you?'

All of Jo's responses to 'Storm Clouds' obliquely indicate the cruel arrangement in progress: stimuli tickling her sensibilities on the

Our view of the conductor's score, Bernard Herrmann's shadow at lower right

beat of a kind of clock. We, however, occupy a more practical state of mind. Hitchcock has ensured that we know where the music is leading, that in a gross, insensitive, horribly implicating way we can foretell the future.

Stammer of truth

Jo's musical engagement has the power to alter our understanding: of her, of the concert hall situation, of the drama itself. She has not raced to the Royal Albert Hall to find her son, has no reason for suspecting he is there or that by going there she will locate him. Nor is it her purpose to abort an assassination, since no clue has warned her such a thing is planned for this place at this time and it is Hank's safety that is of paramount importance. She is there only because Woburn said Buchanan would be present. Buchanan is the object of her quest. And when she spies him he is out of reach, so that her only option is to enter the auditorium (a site of special sensitivities for a person with trained ears).

When she encounters the stranger from Marrakech, can she think, 'Oh, the assassin Louis Bernard warned us about!'? I think, no. In her previous experience, the man seemed gracious, articulate, and educated, not murderous; he is now connected with Hank, issuing a reminder that she must keep her lips sealed (sonically speaking, do nothing). As we hear her destroy the Cantata, we should note that in the event she did *not* heed his warning: not only did she initiate Hank's kidnapping earlier but now, through that prophylactic scream, she has condemned the boy. Further, and quintessential to understanding Hitchcock's purpose: because Jo was absent from Drayton's private music tutorial, she has not learned the assassination cue. The scream is not the result of her waiting for a downbeat anticipated in advance but emerges because storm clouds in Jo have gathered to their bursting point. The bluster of her tact has worn out, and tension can no longer be contained (a point of feeling precisely designed in Benjamin's composition). Just as the vast chorus chants, Jo is 'Finding … release!'

The Assassin dead, Jo is hardly in a position to feel triumph or relief because she has saved anyone's life. More Hitchcockian narrational magic: not only 'anyone's' life but the life of a particular cipher, leader of a country for whom she has no allegiance, in whose embassy her child is hidden *but she does not know it*; a puppet whose bearing acutely suggests emptiness, mental sloth, bureaucratic simplicity. He is surely kind, even avuncular, but is neither Jo's emotional nor Ben's analytical equal. All of this she saw before the concert began, as the Prime Minister made his pompous entrance. How, now, could she wish to greet him and be personally thanked, given that Hank is still lost and in much greater peril than ever?

A saving stammer. The house manager deftly begs her cooperation, his voice the quintessence of Oxbridge babble, quite as though a ritual of state protocol is under way and requires her assent: 'Oh, there they are! Look, do please come over and let the Prime Minister thank you personally, would you? I'm sure he'd like to. It won't take very long, and ... w-would you come along with me and ... and don't be nervous ...' She need merely follow this bubbling toadie for a few steps, merely permit that grateful words be addressed to her. The self-conscious stammering, the preening seriousness of purpose, the desperate sincerity – all instantly aglow in Richard Wattis's brilliant

Richard Wattis (right) had a considerable history of film roles before this very tiny, one-scene bit performance that turns the film

(and considerably experienced) performance – lead gently but inexorably to a moment when the survivor can see the face of his saviour.

Like all vocalisations once the breath is gone, Jo's scream has faded off into history now, heard only – perhaps – in an echoing trace. As she tells the Prime Minister, with remarkable accuracy, 'It wasn't—.' Out of good spirit he replies, 'But it *was*, Madame.' Thanks to this brief meeting, *and for no other reason articulated in the film*, Jo will come to the place where Hank is to be found.

The spirit's voyage

The Royal Albert Hall set piece, boldly conceived to show all of the forces of the choir and orchestra – the conductor's labours, the singers' strain, the soloist's concentration, the opulence of the venue, the audience members' response, the structure of the building, the meticulousness of the score (we get a close shot of the cymbalist's part, showing 171 bars of rest until the cymbal crash in bar 172) – is not, as so many of its viewers and critics have claimed, the climax of *The Man Who Knew Too Much*. It is merely the end of the second act.

At the Prime Minister's embassy, the Draytons are called onto the carpet by the Ambassador, who is, we now learn, the principal director of the assassination plan. 'The target', he informs Drayton, 'merely received a flesh wound in the arm. ... I'm holding a reception here this evening. In a few moments I have to welcome our Prime Minister as my guest of honour when I hoped and expected that he would be totally unable to attend.'

Back at the Albert Hall, Ben and Jo have proceeded to the Green Room, where they learn that Hank is at the embassy, a site to which British authorities have no direct access. But Ben has a clear-headed thought. Phoning the Prime Minister, he says they would be pleased to make a little visit. Jo's 'new friend' is happy to receive them, and so we find ourselves at a lavish soirée, among begowned doyennes and tuxedoed chaperones, all seeming rather confused by the intrusion and suddenly seated to hear a cabaret performance at the grand piano. Ben knew that 'the famous Jo Conway' would

be asked to sing – whenever is she not? – and that during the
entertainment he could scout the building to find Hank.

The quality of Jo's voice singing 'Que Sera, Sera' now becomes
the hero's thread as he enters another labyrinth. As she sings, and
Hank hears her in the upstairs chamber where they have locked
him with Lucy, Ben migrates through the embassy space:[5] out into
the marbled foyer, up the carpeted, flower-laden marble staircase
(lavish, signal bouquets, as at the Savoy; as on the Albert Hall stage).
'That's my mother!' screams Hank to Lucy, and, giving away her
earlier imposture with an ignorant 'Is it, Hank?', she encourages him
protectively to whistle as loud as he can. Up the staircase glides Ben
(the camera at one point replacing him), with Jo's voice growing
subtly dimmer, following and leading him at once. In shots of the
empty staircase, one can easily fathom a ghostly image of that voice
floating up the stairs, the voice as a real and unreal presence. When Jo
modulates to 'We'll Love Again', Ben has arrived at the heights, a
long corridor lined with doors, but the camera leads him to one in
particular where we pause and focus upon the bronzed doorknob with
a suspended breath. He kicks the door in. Hank runs into his arms.

The embassy sitting-room door

Are Jo and her song mere background decoration for the action? Is the motivating force of the film's conclusion finally Ben's sensible navigation through the twisting halls? Jo's voice has become a character in itself, with its own line of movement, and has reached beyond the bounds of her staged performance to contact the sensibility of her trapped son. This is not a mere maternal voice – although, as Hitchcock surely knew, a maternal voice has eminent power – but the voice of music, which sublime form Jo in her persistent purity wholly embodies.

In his composition Hitchcock was classical. Never a cadence without a preparation; never a downbeat without an anticipatory upbeat. The pregnant power of Jo's singing voice and the binding strength that attached her to Hank by virtue of that voice were palpably evident at the Mamounia when mother and son sang 'Que Sera, Sera' and danced together. There it was a childish lullaby; in the embassy, it is a fiery invocation to the gods. But in both cases, when Jo sings, Hank 'sings' with her.

The door to the sacred bed chamber in Hitchcock's first American film, *Rebecca* (1940)

Doris Day with James Stewart; Christopher Olsen; Daniel Gélin; Reggie Nalder

Brenda de Banzie with Bernard Miles; Alexei Bobrinskoy; Mogens Wieth

4 Fathers and Sons

Because *The Man Who Knew Too Much* presents a thoroughgoing
portrait of a woman facing anxious torment with graciousness
and bravery, finally taking action that instigates justice and a
benevolent conclusion, it may well seem a feminist treatment of
heroic femininity in circumstances where femininity is tortured or
at least disempowered. By the mid-1950s in America, practitioners
like Ben McKenna lived and worked in a context founded upon
male privilege, male preferences, and male ascension. A man and his
male child were signal icons of supremacy and potentiality. A wife
was to support, nourish, encourage, and show faith in her husband,
mounting this obligation atop her own aspirations for a career
outside the home.[1]

Hitchcock knew that to picture woman's condition in the
American family – he was a picture-maker even more than a
storyteller – he would ideally need to frame a character who had
suspended a vibrant, significant career to take up the challenges (and
suffer the limitations) of motherhood.[2] The best way to light such
a work would involve presenting a dominant male, even a male–
male line of inheritance. The most revealing vision of Jo would be
embedded in a discourse of fathers and sons.

Consider Ben's revelations to Louis Bernard on the bus as
indicators of the vital weights and balances in the McKenna family,
since the family dialogue is offered as a kind of play-within-
the-play to Bernard's eager eyes and ears. Ben offers information like
a practitioner, while Jo silently and methodically observes. The father
is pedagogical: 'We're just a hundred miles north of the Sahara
Desert, do you realise that, son?' But the mother remains the diffuse,
all-embracing 'Mommy'. This is not only Hank's epithet for Jo.
Operating in a constant state of attentive diagnosis and appreciation,
evaluation and approval, Ben has downgraded his wife from 'the

famous Jo Conway' to a domesticated and, for him, utterly familiar replacement: 'Nobody knows her by any other name, do they?'

With his prediction that Hank will follow in his footsteps, Ben participates in a widespread organisation of occupational inheritance, typical of middle-class American culture in the 1950s, an age of expanding consumerism, relaxation of postwar constraint, testing of newfound prosperity in a former war culture converted for domestic production. For many women, this era promised little but domestic 'security', the confinement of career aspirations inside the cell of 'harmonious' marital obligation – as Simone de Beauvoir had put it in 1949, 'holding away death but also refusing life' (p. 476). Hence Jo's bridling at being denied a continuation of her singing career and eagerness to sing at any opportunity, however cheery or bleak. Ben has been foraging for patients (read, cash), amassing a family (partly as status badge), and applying to the challenges of his daily experience the utile tool of his 'knowledge'. For the child, Ben is a kind of encyclopedia, and when to Bernard's little lecture on Muslim women never removing their veils he cheerily rejoins that they must eat intravenously – 'What a big word for a little boy!' – Hank is showing off, to the stranger but more importantly to his teacher father, in the language Ben taught him. Ben will colonise Hank through discourse; Jo will sing with him: Ben's interaction with Hank will be a lecture, Jo's will be a melody.

With Hank kidnapped, Ben becomes a relentless hunter. If Jo is concerned and anxious at the possibility the child will be hurt or killed, Ben is appropriative, since his valuable treasure has been stolen. The extremity of his desperation is evident in the lengths to which he'll go to regain Hank: 'If he knows anything about this, I'm gonna offer him every penny I have to get Hank back. The Chappell guy's our only hope, now, d'ya understand that, Jo?' says he, packing up in Marrakech. At the taxidermist's, he is brutally explicit, and loses composure: 'Oh, come on, please. Listen to me, will ya? Honestly, if … if … money means anything to ya … uh, I … I'll …'; or 'I don't care who you fellas are gonna kill here in London. All I

want's that boy, I'll take the next aeroplane back to America.'
In the dour little chapel, he becomes openly desperate, barking
the child's name through Drayton's smug front: 'HANK!!! HANK
MCKENNA!!!!'

On the telephone in Buchanan's office, we hear Hank
reacting to Jo's voice, although the shot clearly illustrates both
parents sharing the receiver. 'Mommy? Mommy, is that you?' –
disbelief, perhaps, that he has been offered real contact; or the same
shocked and hungry disconnection any listener might experience in
direct contact with Jo's powerful voice. 'Hank, darling, are you really
all right?' cries she. 'I'm a little scared, Mommy. But I'm all right, I
guess. I miss you, Mommy. I miss you so much!' Choking, she passes
the phone to Ben, who is all business:

BEN   Now Hank, listen to me. Now ... where are you? (Urging): Where
        are you?
HANK   (On phone, off-camera): I didn't mean to make her cry, Daddy.
        But I'm scared and I want to see her.
BEN   Hank ... son, now listen ... tell me where you are.

Neither the maternal emotion nor the paternal direction will prove
of any use here, and the call is abruptly terminated. Jo is adrift on the
cold sea of despair. Ben's canny technique is frustrated.

In a story of a couple and their kidnapped child, however
sociologically astute it may be about gender relations, it is not
structurally necessary to waver from a lucid chain of events involving
the parents' relations with one another or with circumstance.[3]
Ben's fatherly bond to Hank is interesting enough to hold attention
on its own. But Hitchcock inserts a number of *other* father–son links
that must lead us to muse. 'Realism' hardly answers the riddle, since
the scenario is already 'realistic' (Hitchcock can be celebrated for
his sensitive attention to details of setting, period, and psychology).
And Hitchcock never merely decorates. Take, as example, Val Parnell's
ostensibly flip comment at the Savoy, that he had hoped to see which

parent Hank resembled: it's a subtle invocation of inheritance, nature, and nurture, not small talk. *Is* Hank 'gonna make a fine doctor', following his father, or will he follow Jo instead? Or will external circumstances turn him altogether? If it is not decorative or realistic, the connection of Jo's problem to the father–son dyad – and the setting of that dyad among other portrayals of fathers and sons – suggests deeper, more affecting concerns.

Buchanan & Son

After hammering them with threats and imprecations, Buchanan offers a confession to Ben and Jo that sheds light where, for following their story, no light is needed. 'I have got a son of my own,' says he quietly. 'I don't know what *I'd* do.' This is our only glimpse into the stiff agent's private life, indeed the only evidence there is a world for him beyond official investigations. The admission has the strategic effect of humbling him, bringing him closer to the McKennas. If they are destitute and fraught with concern, he can imagine himself in their shoes. The confession also displaces Buchanan from his official capacity, as though to declare in an aside, 'My questioning was routine – my obligation a bureaucratic marker. But my job is only one part of my life, and I am a person beyond the facade I show people who meet me here.' In warming us to himself (more than any other police officer in Hitchcock's oeuvre except Inspector Oxford in *Frenzy*, forced to endure his zany wife's experiments with French cuisine), Buchanan openly invokes staging, in this way mirroring Jo's perspective and anticipating the assassination choreography that will follow. He sees the dividing line between rule books and moral codes. Does he think his son will be a fine policeman or does he, with Jo, believe 'Que sera, sera'?

Ambrose and Ambrose

Older and younger Ambrose Chappell make a comical pair, the son being so much more sententious than the father. Sagacious Senior is the first target Ben encounters inside the shop, but it becomes clear

to the old man Ben needs a fresher Ambrose. 'Now father ... now ...
why don't you go and have a nice rest, eh?' says Junior, with the sort
of patronising tone wise old men are accustomed to hearing from
the inexperienced. 'I have centuries of rest ahead of me, thank you,'
says Senior curtly but roundly.[4] Now young Ambrose must try to
make sense of this strange American's queries and wild demands:
(1) that he heard about Chappell from a man in Marrakech, Louis
Bernard (unknown); (2) that Bernard told him about Chappell just
before dying ('This man is ... dead?'); (3) that young Ambrose surely
knows Bernard is dead 'just as well as I do. Now I've come here with
a business proposition. I don't see how you can turn it down' – a
cutaway to a member of the taxidermist's staff stuffing a leopard.
(What, this bizarre man wants to make arrangements to have his
Moroccan friend stuffed?)

As a hopelessly misleading – if entertaining and optically
fascinating – adventure that kept promising to bear fruit, the
taxidermy shop would have done quite well on its own, an
uncomprehending proprietor making clear that our hero had found
the wrong spot. The obedient, diligent staff members could operate
just as well with one Ambrose directing them as two. Why present
the viewer with a father–son combination? Certainly, the Chappells
represent a doubling: doubles and echoes, doubles as phantoms.
Is there more to them still?

Does one Chappell offer a comment the other does not?
The only point of difference between father and son – one that
requires the presence of both – is the son's brazen attempt to put his
father out to pasture: a clue in its own right? The weight of a father's
power is something a son may grow to lift – or brush – away; Youth
might choose to displace Age before Age has readied himself for
displacement. The theme is the transfer of power across generations.
Mythically, young Ambrose's overleaping calls up the ritual of the
Priest of Nemi described by Sir James George Frazer in *The Golden
Bough*, in which a younger man slays his predecessor in order to
come into full maturity and take his place.[5] The self-aware old

Ambrose Chappell demonstrates one way to handle the burgeoning power of a protégé; Ben's continual definition, instruction, and effective limitation of Hank demonstrate another. To be in power is to hold onto the reins. ('He can spell haemoglobin. 'Course he has a little trouble with words like dog and cat.')

Patricide

But once more to note, Hitchcock always gives a preparation before a cadence.[6] Could Buchanan's invocation of his own fatherhood and the strange father–son relationship between the Chappells be set-ups for something more culminating, more troubling, more dramatic? The idea of the son pushing the father out of the picture finds its place in a truly stunning moment late in the film, one composed entirely as an icon. We are in the ambassadorial study at the embassy, the room arrayed with leathered furniture, elegant polished wooden tables, warming lamps, and artful landscapes in gilded frames on the walls. The sepulchral silence is broken only by the Ambassador berating Drayton for the botched assassination.

We take position adjacent to Drayton in front of the ornate wooden desk, with the Ambassador casting his cutting gaze in our direction from behind it, pomposity riding his ruddied face so that, as we see him from below, he seems to 'bellow' with his furious, slickly maned head, scornful lips, and a forest-green sash slashing his starched white shirt.

Behind the Ambassador's back is a huge framed portrait, clearly visible as his 'background'.

This is the Prime Minister, head proudly erect, shirtfront boasting a flaming red sash, eyes (thoughtfully or thoughtlessly) glazed, balding pate suggestive of excessive maturity and decline.[7] (If it is unsurprising to find such a portrait in an embassy, why, still, did Hitchcock instruct Robert Burks to construct a shot to display it over the Ambassador's shoulder?)

The picture – Hitchcock's picture: Ambassador plus Prime Minister in official stance behind him – clearly enunciates what is

nowhere else in the film told: that the one is father to the other.
That the planned assassination was a patricide. 'Father': in blood, or
through bureaucratic arrangement, or both – the elegant ambiguity
of the moment opens all these possibilities without offering a clue
toward resolution. The firm jaw, the eyes, the proud brow are
mimicked, inherited by the Ambassador, as the frame bluntly shows.
And what is patricide but the termination of history? The erasure
of beginnings, earliest formations: a change of life. In capitalism,
patricide is an everyday routine, the commitment to progress at any
cost implying constant renovation, constant faithlessness to the past,
a pervading optimism that blots out memory. In this light, consider
again the pre-capitalist labyrinth of Morocco presented early in the
film: is it a trap or a paradise?

Jo's tendentious position in her family, her long-standing career,
her vocal power, and her ability to love have been motored and
threaded by an intergenerational male rivalry, a young and puissant
man's quest for the power his elderly parent retains and refuses to
cede. Ambrose and Ambrose Chappell were hints in advance – clear
and sharp, but placed in such a way that their tonal weight would not
outbalance the weight of events to follow. In screaming, Jo did more
than save the life of a high-ranking civil servant. She saved a father

Patricide

from his own son. With her own son still in a formative state, and through a considerably more lyrical approach, is she doing the reverse?

Drayton

Finally, Drayton. This is a man without a son, indeed a man with no regard for sons. He is willing, on orders, to bring Hank down to the embassy basement for a strangling. Without regard for even his wife (holding Ben and Hank at gunpoint, he intends to find the nearest taxi rank outside and be gone, leaving her to face justice alone), he fails to notice, or finds immaterial, her own attachment to the boy, who has become, at least for a breath, her surrogate child. Able easily to mask himself – a soil expert, a preacher, a thug – Drayton must wonder, just as we do, who he is before and beneath the masquerade. In a fast-moving world, he takes his money where he can find it, and takes his orders from whoever stands above, mercenary to the core. Is this why, offered a few moments of free speech in front of his

Stresses of fatherhood: Hitchcock rehearsing the Ambrose Chapel cosh

congregation, he chooses to invoke adversity? Is he living in a turgid prison of the self, 'harassed and perplexed, by disappointment and by cruelties beyond our control'? He mocks the Assassin, suggesting the fancy box at the Albert Hall might lend him 'an air of respectability, if that is possible'. But could this fatherless and childless villain be referring to himself, a man who, no matter the cloak under which he hides, cannot find the son who will follow him today, and lead him tomorrow?

5 In Arcady

'Et in Arcadia ego' is inscribed on a stone column supporting a skull being considered by a pair of young shepherds in the Guercino painting from around 1620. The idea – that 'disillusionment awaits all attempts at pastoral evasion' (Freccero, pp. 120–1) – is recaptured about twenty years later by Poussin, in his *Arcadian Shepherds*. Guercino's sylvan glade and the worn stones of his column suggest temporality stopped in nature, which has reached its fullest burgeoning at a moment of perfect, now frozen, ripeness. The boys apotheosise this flowering and stillness, this *sense of the moment*, and they are framed in a setting that suggests richness, beauty, incessant springing forth: what may seem *all the goodness of the world*. This is the context in which Death announces, in muted tones, 'I am here, too.'

The Man Who Knew Too Much emerges from a profoundly philosophical, even religious sensibility concerned with man's experience and place in the universe. While Hitchcock always conjured his films for a wide and excitable reception, it is only in the most superficial way that they can be said to have popular appeal as

The music of vision

thrillers, suspense epics, or excursions into the macabre, by which epithets he permitted his work and persona to be advertised. This film is no simple tale of kidnapping in an exotic clime. The exoticism, as I have suggested, has implications about labyrinthine, premodern experience, the torsion of the marketplace and the (causative) inevitability of the chase. In its curious exotic evening, we find replicated the windings of the ear and the mysteries of the voice. The kidnapping opens the issue of generational continuity. And throughout, the film is suffused with musical provocation, even beyond Benjamin's rich Cantata and the Evans/ Livingston pop hits, a group of rich and chilling Bernard Herrmann cues, the pathetic rendition of 'The Portents' in the chapel, one authentic composed Arabic music riff and a further nine drawn from material pre-recorded in Africa, and three items of chamber music in a minor key composed for the restaurant scene. Follow the story, certainly, but gaze past its surfaces.

The Royal Albert Hall, our first Arcadian glimpse, is a civil structure designed expressly to facilitate acoustic experience. Matching the visual interest of Hitchcock's images, with the shining instruments and beautifully decorated platform, comes a rich and piercing sound (emphasised with trombones and tympani), the cymbalist's culminating crash artfully mixed by the sound engineers with the humming motor of the Casablanca–Marrakech bus,[1] so that the vehicle is transformed into an echo of the orchestral gesture, an instrumentation. The action thus become orchestral, we are cued for special attention to matters acoustic, not just the pained whine of the bus but the little boy's chatter, the squealing brakes as the driver swerves and the veil is yanked off, the staccato bark of the angry Arab's voice, the calming suavity of Bernard's response: instrumentations all. Action flows through unfamiliar spaces built for differing resonances (the marketplace, the hotel room, the twilit city), continuing the symphonic quality of the film's development.

Let us entertain a further, aesthetic consideration of the Cantata performance that provides so thrilling an interest for Jo and Ben struggling to save their child.[2] What does the concert *look like*, as Hitchcock shows it? While in his 1934 version of the film – 'the work of a talented amateur',[3] as he described it to François Truffaut (p. 94) – the same piece (but shorter by some two minutes) was used, the cinematographic array for 1956 was more sumptuous and more carefully plotted. Hitchcock met at the Albert Hall with his designer and cinematographer, as well as Herrmann, to elaborate the shots virtually bar by bar (with lenses ranging from 28 to 75mm[4]), intending a chain of splendid depictions while the sumptuous music flowed: the full stage, performing forces tactically arrayed; the radiant soloist and energetic conductor; the singers, section by section, seen in whites and blacks from every conceivable angle; the mesmerised audience.[5] Various musicians are singled out, notably the cymbalist patiently – or anxiously[6] – counting through his scoreful of rests with shining tools at the ready. In this shot and in a fleeting vision of the conductor's score is denoted laborious collaboration, a shared system of tonal division and metronomically counted time deftly collecting the labour of disparate minions into a single coherent (transcendent) unity. The careful management of productive forces – willing, gifted, attentively devoted specialists of many kinds – marshalling ability and desire in a tightly integrated presentation for the pleasure of thousands (who have placed themselves silently within earshot) constitutes a utopian picture. As we hear the wafting lyric and experience the glittering vision of the music-makers, we may see how film, as Hitchcock said, 'approaches nearest to music and the ballet' ('Films', p. 165) – a relation discernible from the Marrakech marketplace chase to the embassy's echoing halls.

Release

To address 'Storm Clouds' as metaphor is perhaps to reach deepest inside it. When people collaborate toward harmony (that is, *goodness*), some regularising system constrains and liberates their action. The result is a form of beauty, beneficence, and boundary – a garden – in which experience is rarefied and elevated, time enriched, and the weight of action diminished in the light of creation until gravity seems non-existent, obligations disappear, torments and agonies are sweetened. Thus is the concert hall a stand-in for the social fabric more broadly, and the Cantata sequence a variation upon that special locus enunciated by Guercino (and other painters to follow, from Lorrain and Hondecoeter to Courbet and Cézanne). Heard and seen, the musical gesture is 'Arcadian'.

If the opening credits and Cantata sequence, taken together, indicate the artistic ideal, humanity's potential for goodness, still, 'Et in Arcadia ego'. The worm, having entered, waits to grow. Or, as Hitchcock sees it, within our affairs evil, too, gains a place, our fate being to live in its presence, not banish it. Thus, the painful delicacy of that little lecture we attend for our amusement and education, with pedantic Drayton taking time out from dressing up to teach his Assassin the music according to which he will time his work. This is upstairs at the chapel in a modest, not quite shabby room: warm lamplight, a small bookcase, a chest of drawers, and at the centre, plugged into an overhead light fixture that sports a pleasing stained-glass shade, a record player with Drayton's vinyl disk spinning. 'Music's less in your line than marksmanship,' he intones. 'Now if you listen, I'm going to play you the exact moment – *Lucy gulps* – at which you can shoot. So listen carefully.' This is a call for the audience's attention more than the Assassin's, since already, by his darting eyes and smirking mouth, he shows he is listening quite as carefully as one could hope. Drayton carefully places the needle and we hear the final splendid bars of the Benjamin.

A touching and disturbing pedagogy: that a musical downbeat and a pistol shot could come together. More: that the pistol could be a musical instrument like any other, an instrument like the ones we push air through or strike with the hand or saw with taut strings. There is violence in producing musical sound, but violence shaped and organised. Now the organised violence of killing will become musical, too. 'Et in Arcadia ego.'

'We'll have it once more,' says Drayton. 'Listen for the crash of the cymbals.' (Hitchcock to Truffaut: 'The reason why the cantata record is played twice is to prevent any confusion in the viewer's mind about the events that are to follow. I've often found that a suspense situation is weakened because the action is not sufficiently clear' [p. 92].) Teacher now drops his hand like a conductor (although with the fingers curled as in gripping a gun) to make a clear downbeat on the crash of cymbals (as the choir hits the second, fatal syllable of the word 'Release!').

The twin lessons do not suffice for Drayton. Once the Assassin has left for the concert, he savours for himself the brilliance of melding murder with music, setting the needle a third time so that the cymbal crash and the word 'Release' can titillate him privately: privately, yet in our presence, so that now, having learned the mechanism of the trick in this tranquil moment, we can appreciate it in advance – implicated by Hitchcock's craft to anticipate the crash that will kill. Through the interconnection of Drayton's solitary pleasure with the audience's dark enjoyment at this instant, Hitchcock reveals our intimacy with the source of evil in the garden. It is not us. *Yet it is with us*, lurking behind our compassion and our appetite for truth and beautiful form.

The Assassin is doubled in the mirror; Drayton's dickey, covering his clean shirt, mirrors the Assassin's holstered gun, a tool of violence. Lucy holds her breath

In the concert hall, something marvellous happens. The harmonic integration of the musical performance is fractured, shut down at the perfect juncture not by a killing but by the intrusion of quite another musical voice: high-pitched, wholly serious, desperate beyond estimation, excessive even, and characteristic. When Jo screams, she brings to the moment a truly human musical utterance, a rhythmic and harmonic outpouring, what Herbert Read called the 'true voice of feeling'. She works not from the imposed score but from the heart as she sings out her release on the upbeat to the cymbal crash, not the downbeat: otherwise, the Prime Minister would be dead. Her climax is therefore off the notation.

Here, Hitchcock points to the discrepancy – and mutual involvement – between innocence and complicity. A sharp example: the conductor's score, with frenetic sixteenth-note passages in the violins as the climax builds, now magnified onscreen and Herrmann lost in beating it out with the orchestra.[7] The conductor has the entire musical composition laid out before him, instrument by instrument; he can see where the Cantata is going and with what sense of urgency (sixteenth-note passages are radically different from whole or half notes); and finally, he can count his way toward the conclusion. In his film role as conductor of 'The London Symphony Orchestra and

Covent Garden Chorus, with Barbara Howitt,[8] in a performance
of the "Storm Clouds" Cantata by Arthur Benjamin and
D. B. Wyndham-Lewis', Bernard Herrmann is assiduously and
devotedly *leading his forces* to the moment when they will accompany
– cover and trigger – the Prime Minister's death.[9] But neither he,
nor the musicians, nor the Prime Minister know this is happening.
Herrmann onscreen is thus innocent of the murder he is about to help
someone commit, yet at the same time, because he is an indisputable
aide, morally culpable.

(Morally, not legally.)

The conductor – the film-maker's 'effigy' – will be responsible for
the killing as though he were an assassin himself. Waving his arms, he
cocks a kind of trigger, or energises a kind of timer. Jo's inexpressible
power lies in her ability to vocalise a stop to the progression of the
performance: stopping the orchestra, stopping the scheduled music
with her felt 'music'. While anyone can technically do this at any time,
listeners' forbearance in holding back is part of their contribution
to the moment, and so, in this case, their contribution to the murder
plot. Etiquette as violence. By devotedly playing or devotedly listening,
everyone contributes to a scheme Drayton has arranged (Hitchcock
has arranged it so that Drayton can arrange) to mechanise the
murder. (This is death by composition.) If the Assassin succeeds,
everyone in the auditorium will be his partner. The Prime Minister,
too, joins in, loving listener that he is, with a childish grin etched on
his blank face.

But there is a single exception to the rule (just as in the sacred
garden of Arcady a single skull). At the rehearsal, when Drayton
smugly promised, 'No one will know,' the Assassin sagely responded,
'No one … except one.' We must wonder, 'Who?' When first I
saw this film, I know that in my childishness I took the Assassin
to be indicating the victim himself: the Prime Minister would bear
knowledge. At the time, I found this thought chilling enough, but
have spent decades since discovering its disconcerting limitations.
With a bullet directly to the heart (the Assassin's intent, and the

reason behind the Draytons' choosing a man of exceptional skill), the Prime Minister would feel and know nothing. His world would simply cease.

The Assassin might have meant himself; but he could be in no position to *know*, rushing out rather than enjoying his bullseye.

There is only one the Assassin could be invoking, one or One. As he speaks, he touches on his own moral vulnerability through his belief that there is a God who will see his action and know the full depth of its consequence. As God placed the snake in the garden, he is aware of the snake's temptation. For the Assassin, then, the quotidian rationales of money-earning, political contrivance, and social impropriety will all evanesce in the face of the morally implicating act for which Drayton, wolf in sheep's clothing, has rehearsed him. Drayton's musician-murderer is to hide himself in the conductor's garden, a musician among musicians, knowing that if no one knows what he is about to do, it will nevertheless *be known* that he has done it.

A coda

The film ends on a happy – or at least what seems a wholly just – note. Escorted with his trembling son down the embassy staircase at the point of Drayton's gun, with Jo's crooning voice getting louder and louder the closer they come to the foyer, Ben suddenly shoves the brute, who rolls down the steps, triggering the gun and killing himself. Abject Lucy gapes from a high railing. The crowd in the salon, having heard the noise, races into the lobby, as does Jo. In the hubbub, Hank falls into his mother's arms.

A more conventional approach to such a story would have ended here, with Hank hugging 'Mommy' in close-up, his father peaceful at the side.[10] Instead, the camera lingers on the staircase, watching from a distance, and Hitchcock boldly takes us past this moment to:

The Savoy Hotel.

Back to that too comfortable room, where poor Val and Helen Parnell, Cindy Fontaine, and Jan Peterson have been waiting all day and now lie in stupor upon the smartly upholstered furniture like a quartet of rag dolls, intruders entirely outside the tale.

In burst the three McKennas, grinning from ear to ear, and Ben announces that he is sorry they were gone so long but they had to go over and pick up Hank! Smashing non-diegetic orchestral punch as the guests sit up stunned and the film is done.

There is a delightful conceit to this 'sympathy for the strangers', now bored to tears, awaiting the vision of the child with his parents they have been longing to see. While in one incarnation we have been accompanying Ben and Jo on their adventure, in another we have lingered at the Savoy, because seeing the kidnapping, the assassination, the concert, and the escape from death have not been our principal desire: were it so, this finale moment would be superfluous in the extreme. As we align with the sleepy quartet, a neat reunion portrait – two parents beaming with joy and their child between them – is the appropriate clincher, the accurate punchline to the joke of a day's tedious confusion. Yet, why would we align with – why would we now be seeing – Parnell & Co.? Giving this coda a second glance brings to *The Man Who Knew Too Much*, I think, a startling illumination.

The concluding point, as Hitchcock shows it, is not that Ben and Jo have been reunited with Hank, although they have, but that Ben (who dominates this finale) needs to show that reunion (as though on a stage). Had it been enough for Hitchcock, he would have shot the family portrait among the diplomats at the embassy, where all the key actors were already present (in a beautiful setting). The diplomats, however, lack the standing that Parnell and his chums possess, not in their own eyes, perhaps, nor in the viewer's necessarily, but in the eyes of the man who knows too much. It is in front of *these paragons of show business* that the family must pose.

'Show business' means something to Ben McKenna that it need hardly mean to his wife, who *is* and *was* show business of another kind, and needs no hints as to what performance implies or requires. (Casting Doris Day was signal for Hitchcock in making the film, because although she had made plenty of films, she remained a singer/celebrity more than a movie star.) For Ben, life itself is show business. He is constantly aware of being on show, being viewed, being estimated and weighed, being evaluated against standards of accomplishment. He's not just a doctor, he's at the Good Samaritan Hospital in Indianapolis. He didn't just carry out wartime activities in North Africa, he 'liberated' the place. He isn't just the father of a young boy, he is the progenitor of a future 'fine doctor'. He doesn't just bring Jo to London, he contacts Val Parnell in advance to arrange for a hotel room (and Parnell arranges for a fan club to be waiting at the airport). He can't make himself comfortable on the soft cushions of the restaurant, or eat squab with his hand no matter how hungry he is, because it all just doesn't look right. Ben always gives the appearance of having the right attitude – in short, he performs his experience.

In the final moment, Hitchcock shows Ben as a man who cannot allow that he and his partner might be seen for what they actually are, two well-meaning innocents who (culpably) gave their son away. Nor can he be thought the kidnapper who took Jo from show business in order to bear this child who was lost. Hank must be not only touched but exhibited, openly and physically, to people who are in the business of making and appreciating exhibitions. What better audience for a little stage work, after all, than a pack of entertainers, who know a good act when they see one! Ben has recouped his family and mounted his production. Jo, having expended her voice in the service of all this, has fallen silent.

So it is that the very last moment of *The Man Who Knew Too Much* is very like the first. A stage especially lit on which an explicit performance is in play. A position of viewing that permits our consciousness of the staged performance *as such*, not an acted reality caught by the film-maker's camera but an acted *act* caught along with its audience by that camera. At the beginning we had a cymbalist, with two matching instruments poised beside his ears. At the end, the child is the musician in the middle, with one glowing 'symbol' on each side.

Family unity is itself a lavish garden, another Arcadian form. We interpret the child, perhaps especially this sprightly one, as a sign of natural goodness, a springing forth into golden light. But even in the perfect American family, as *The Man Who Knew Too Much* shows, the spirit of contrivance and guilt has sneaked in. 'We had better explain ourselves,' rather than, 'We are here.' And more: a perfectly equivocal trap as Ben gets caught in that interminable game – revealed in his last line – of knowing something innocent others do not know. Not death, perhaps, but a startling intimation of negativity has now infected Ben McKenna's clan, and for all the breadth of his medical knowledge he will have to turn to his wife to find a cure.

Emergency exit

Notes

Chapter 1

1 'My role was dubbed by an actor with a serious voice, who had the French accent I had succeeded in losing,' Gélin recounted to me.

2 In the mid-1950s, 'cosmetics were one of the massive growth areas as [American] consumer spending increased' (Ritchie, p. 737).

3 I am indebted to Abdelwahed Boutahor for help with the translation.

4 The carriage was purchased in Morocco and shipped to Hollywood for rear-projection photography (Bumstead to Pereira).

5 Ms Day was offered her entire wardrobe at 50 per cent discount, when shooting was done (Caffey).

6 On Hitchcock's explicit instruction, the song begins with Day humming.

7 Founded in 1940 and expanded in 1948, McDonald's went into franchising in 1952 (Halberstam, p. 159).

8 Bernard here speaks like a film-maker or editor, whose concern for timing often leads to counting frames.

9 Although Hitchcock was unaware of this when he cast him, Reggie Nalder (Alfred Reginald Natzler) had been a singer and ballet dancer in Vienna (Coleman, Personal correspondence, 19 July). 'He has this terrific face. That's why he was cast,' the agent Carl Forest told me, adding, 'He talked with his hands.' The facial burns were from radiation after surgery, I was informed by Donald Spoto, who knew him. Irene Hayman of the Paul Kohner agency (Nalder's representatives) recollected, 'We called Reggie "The Freak", with extreme affection. He probably knew it. We used the German, "Die Fratze". … He was as weird as he looked – spoke in a whisper. … He would sit at Pupi's on the Strip. All the refugee gentlemen and ladies sat there. He was always there, looking for a Viennese coffee house.'

10 Handling the Moroccan extras was a nightmare. 'Poor [assistant director Howard] Joslin is going to be worn down to a skeleton because, unfortunately, his two French assistants are almost useless, and it is quite a picture to watch Joslin setting the action for a couple of hundred people and speaking only English' (Erickson to Caffey, 19 May). 'It has been very difficult working here,' Bumstead explained about Marrakech, 'because of the language barrier. Your message usually goes from English to French to Arabic and when they finally get your message it's nothing like you intended it to be' (Bumstead to Pereira). There were two other 'serious' problems facing the crew, Erickson wrote: the intense heat, and Ramadan, during which, because they were permitted very little food and water, the extras were exhausted (Erickson to Caffey, 6 May).

11 From the Production Code office, Geoffrey Shurlock wrote coyly to Paramount on 12 May 1955 warning that 'the scenes of the man with the knife in his back should be handled with extreme delicacy, to avoid offense' (PCA file). Other PCA concerns included the kidnapping of a child and the portrayal of Drayton as a bogus minister.

Chapter 2

1 Developed by Loren Ryder at Paramount in 1953, VistaVision passed film laterally through the camera with eight sprocket holes. The resultant negative image was two and a half times the size of normal 35mm negatives, and permitted, especially on very large screens, astonishingly bright, crisp, grain-free, and 'realistic' imagery.

2 'Need small abandoned type, Protestant church; forget Gothic design,' Herbert Coleman had stipulated on 5 April 1955 (*Man Who Knew Too Much*, Coleman file). The chapel exterior was shot at St Saviour's Church in Brixton Hill, with complex arrangements being negotiated for the repair of the belfry (that would appear in the exteriors), Filwite, the production company, agreeing to donate £75 to the church's funds (Hartwright). The close-up of Ben peering down at the crowd is a studio shot.

3 See Weis for a detailed analysis of the acoustic structure of this scene.

4 I am grateful to C. T. Gillin for information about Ambrose.

5 Effigies are addressed later by Hitchcock in *Psycho* (1960) and referenced obliquely by the 'frozen' rendition of a dead father in both *Suspicion* (1941) and *The Birds* (1963).

6 Betty Baskcomb, the only cast member who had also appeared in Hitchcock's 1934 version.

7 Herbert Coleman shared with me Peggy Robertson's recollection that Alma Reville had suggested this hymn (Personal correspondence, 13 July 1995).

8 The battle against adversity betokens in some ways a search for 'respectability', thus the working-class nature of this congregation (for more on this social class, see Kynaston, *Family*, p. 155).

Chapter 3

1 The song was composed and completed within about half an hour, after Livingston and Evans came away from watching Joseph L. Mankiewicz's *The Barefoot Contessa* (1954). Seeing the phrase 'Che sera, sera' etched in a cave, they hastily scribbled it on a napkin (Livingston).

2 Another Livingston/Evans composition, 'Holy Gee', was rejected by the ultra-religious Day, and changing the title to 'Holy Cow' didn't make a difference (Livingston).

3 Utilising a familiar *lazzo* of Jackie Gleason, similarly well known at the same time.

4 Day would have understood such honesty: her own ten-year-old son had travelled to Marrakech with her.

5 The hallway and staircase were shot at Park Lane House.

Chapter 4

1 Postwar sexism has been discussed at length, relatively recently, by such scholars as Elaine Tyler May and Elaine Showalter. Seven years after the release of *Manmuch* (Coleman and Hitchcock's pet abbreviation for the film), Betty Friedan's *The Feminine Mystique* forcefully put American women's condition on the public cultural agenda.

2 A character not unlike the brilliant scenarist, editor, and film-maker Alma Reville, whom he had married in 1926.

3 A very good example of tight family focus in a kidnap story is Alex Segal's *Ransom!*, released by MGM earlier in 1956.

4 Echoing the words of Daniel Touchett in Chapter 18 of Henry James's *Portrait of a Lady*.

5 In *Invitation to the Dance* (1956), Gene Kelly's choreography of the harlequinade shows precisely this routine, with a tightrope walker thrown down from his high perch by a Fool type, who leaps over him. And a film Hitchcock would have known well, F. W. Murnau's *The Last Laugh* (1924), has an extended passage in which an older hotel employee is abruptly replaced by a younger one through the mechanism of a revolving door.

6 In the chapel sequence, at the conclusion of the sung hymn there is *no cadence* ['A-men!'] where we might reasonably expect to hear one. In Hitchcock, the cadence is filmic, ultimately optical, not a set of musical chords.

7 '*The Man Who Knew Too Much* was banned by the censors in Burma during March last,' Paramount Vice-President Luigi Luraschi wrote to Hitchcock on 5 September 1957. '… confidentially we understand that the attempted assassination of a Prime Minister and the kidnapping of a child were the two main points which were objected to … As you know, the entire Cabinet of Ministers (I think seven of them including the Prime Minister) were shot dead in Rangoon city by a gang of Burmese nationals several years ago and the Board there is rather reluctant to reconsider its decision' (Luraschi).

Chapter 5

1 'At the very outset, the ring of the cymbals should carry over into the whine of the tires on the roadway,' Hitchcock dictated in an explicit note (*Man Who Knew Too Much*, Dubbing file).

2 Wyndham-Lewis's original lyric 'Yet save the child' was altered by Herrmann to 'Yet stood the trees' for this film. Hitchcock knew that watching Ben and Jo's urgency would be a sufficient invocation of the missing 'child', and that the apparent coincidence of the choir intoning about a 'child' might seem heavy-handed or false.

3 For more on the relationship between the two films, see Pomerance, 'Looking up'. John Michael Hayes, hired to write the 1956 version, was given careful instruction by Hitchcock *not to see* the original film: 'I'm going to tell you the story and you'll write it' (Hayes communication).

4 The 28mm is a wide-angle lens that would have condensed more lateral material into a shot but produced some shape-warping; the 75mm is a long lens that would have drawn the background forward, cramping the depth of field. Hitchcock was clearly interested in varying the graphic look and in providing different kinds of information to the viewer at critical junctures, such as in the long-lens shot of the conductor seen from the rear of the orchestra, with the separated, readied cymbals framing the screen at left and right.

5 The Albert Hall shoot was high-pressured. 'Some of our crews have worked 24 hours and longer without a rest break,' Erickson signalled. 'We worked until 11 o'clock last night … in order to finish the choir' (Erickson to Caffey, 7 June).

6 An orchestral musician regaled me with a percussionist's horror story: during Shostakovich's 7th Symphony, counting out the bars before his one and only bass drumbeat, to be sounded at triple-fortissimo, he suddenly realised that many bars before, the 4/4 time signature had changed to 2/2! His powers of computation failing him, he came in one bar early with a thump entirely 'offbeat'. Like legion players in orchestral percussion sections, Hitchcock's cymbalist is indubitably worried about committing such a gaffe; he sits in terror. **7** There is, incidentally, no such actual passage in the Benjamin conductor's score: this has been invented for camera. **8** Howitt was an old friend of Arthur Benjamin's, at the time singing supporting roles at Covent Garden with the young Joan Sutherland (Duker). **9** Herrmann is the figure in all the photographed Albert Hall shots, but when the Cantata was being rehearsed and recorded for sound at London's Festival Hall (26–8 May), the conductor, at least some of the time, was Herrmann's friend Richard Arnell. The Albert Hall photography some days later – the musicians shot separately from the audience – was meticulously pre-planned, as the company had access to the location for only a few days. See Pomerance, 'Finding Release'. **10** See, for just one example, the concluding moment of reunification in Steven Spielberg's *Empire of the Sun* (1987), which is a kind of homage to this Hitchcockian scene.

Credits
1 Alfred Hitchcock, James Stewart, and Lew Wasserman in partnership.

Credits

**The Man Who Knew
Too Much**
USA/1956

Directed by
Alfred Hitchcock
Produced by
Alfred Hitchcock (via
Filwite Associates[1])
Associate Producer
Herbert Coleman
Screenplay by
John Michael Hayes
Based on a story by
Charles Bennett
D. B. Wyndham-Lewis

© 1956 Filwite
Productions Inc
Production Company
Paramount Pictures
(Paramount Production
10336)
Production Manager
Frank Caffey
**Assistant Production
Manager**
Hugh Brown
**Unit Production
Manager**
Clarence O. 'Doc'
Erickson
1st Assistant Director
Howard Joslin
2nd Assistant Directors
Ralph Axness
Ned Dobson
Casting
Eddie Morse
Director of Photography
Robert Burks

Camera Operator
Leonard South
Assistant Cameraman
Paul Uhl
Colour Consultant
Richard Mueller
Art Director
Henry Bumstead
Process Photography
Farciot Edouart
Stills
Ken Lobben
Grip
Darrell Turnmire
Set Decoration
Arthur Krams
**Technical Advisor
(English)**
Constance Willis
**Technical Advisor
(Arabic)**
Abdelhaq Chraibi
Editor
George Tomasini
Assistant Cutter
Sam Vitale
Script Supervisor
Constance Willis
Script Clerk
Charles Morton
Costumes
Edith Head
Make-up Supervision
Wally Westmore
Sound Recording
Paul Franz and Gene
Garvin, with Henry
Keener
'Storm Cloud Cantata'
Arthur Benjamin
D. B. Wyndham-Lewis

Performed by
The London Symphony
Orchestra and Covent
Garden Chorus
Conducted by
Bernard Herrmann (and
Richard Arnell)
Soloist
Barbara Howitt
Music Scoring
Bernard Herrmann
Songs by
Jay Livingston
Ray Evans
Stage Engineer
William Pillar
Mike Grip
Frank Carroll
Gaffer
Vic Jones
Electrician
Adolph Froelich
Script Consultant
Angus MacPhail
Choreography
Nick Castle
**Teacher for Mstr
Olsen**
Catherine Barton
Publicity
David Hanna
Art Sarno
Props
Walter Broadfoot
Neil Wheeler
Wardrobe Woman
Lee Forman
Wardrobe Man
Leonard Mann
Hairdresser
Virginia Darcy

Make-up
Dan Greenway
**Transparency
Cameraman**
W. Wallace Kelley

CAST
(in order of appearance)
**London Symphony
Orchestra**
orchestra
Charlie Quirk
cymbalist
James Stewart
Dr Ben McKenna
Doris Day
Jo Conway McKenna
Christopher Olsen
Hank McKenna
Mahin S. Shahrivar
Arab wife
Abdelhaq Chraibi
Arab husband
Lou Krugman
Arab man
Daniel Gélin
Louis Bernard
F. de Valorbe
concièrge, Hôtel de la
Mamounia
R. Ingarao
policeman
Bernard Miles
Edward Drayton
Brenda de Banzie
Lucy Drayton
Edward Manouk
room service waiter
Reggie Nalder
man at door (The
Assassin)
Peter Camlin
head waiter, Moroccan
restaurant

Gladys Holland
Louis Bernard's
companion
**Louis Mercier
Anthony Warde
Albert Carrier**
gendârmes in
marketplace
Yves Brainville
Chef Inspecteur,
Marrakech
Harry Fine
Inspector Edington
Betty Baskcomb
Edna
Noel Willman
Inspector Woburn
Ralph Truman
Chief Inspector
Buchanan
Donald Lawton
Savoy desk clerk
Alix Talton
Helen Parnell
Hillary Brooke
Jan Peterson
Carolyn Jones
Cindy Fontaine
Alan Mowbray
Val Parnell
Richard Wordsworth
Ambrose Chappell Jr
George Howe
Ambrose Chappell Sr
**Frank Atkinson
John Barrard
Mayne Lynton
Liddell Peddieson**
workmen in
taxidermist's shop
Leo Gordon
chauffeur
Patrick Aherne
English handyman

Guy Verney
embassy footman
Milton Frome
embassy butler
Walter Gotell
guard
Elsa Palmer
kitchen cook
Betty Baskcomb
scullery maid
Barry Keegan
Patterson
**Eric Snowden
Patrick Whyte**
Special Branch officers
Joe Wadham
police driver
F. G. Hudd
taxi driver
**Janet Bruce
Alma Taylor**
Albert Hall box-office
women
Lloyd Lamble
Albert Hall general
manager
Richard Wattis
Albert Hall assistant
manager
Wolf Frees
Prime Minister's aide
Alexei Bobrinskoy
Prime Minister
Richard Marner
Ambassador's aide
Mogens Wieth
Ambassador
Pauline Farr
Ambassador's wife
Clifford Buckton
Sir Kenneth Clarke
Enid Lindsey
Lady Clarke

Arthur Ridley
ticket collector
John O'Malley
uniformed attendant
Barbara Burke
Miss Benson
Naida Buckingham
Janet MacFarlane
ladies in the audience
Alex Frazer
man
Allen Zeidman
assistant manager
John Marshall
Ambassador's butler

Leslie Newport
police inspector at
Albert Hall
Peter Williams
police sergeant
Harold Kasket
embassy butler
Ralph Neff
henchman

Pat Ryan
stand-in for James
Stewart
Ted Mapes
James Stewart double
for roof shots

Nora Miller
stand-in for Doris Day

Shot on Eastmancolor
negative in the
VistaVision format
(1.85:1), printed by
Technicolor®

Released in the USA
1 June 1956

Running time:
110 minutes

Bibliography

HER = Margaret Herrick Library, Academy of Motion Picture Arts and Sciences, Beverly Hills.

Bumstead, Henry, Letter to Hal Pereira regarding set designs, 18 May 1955. Paramount Production Records, file 12, HER.

———, Personal conversation, 28 December 1995.

Caffey, Fran, Memorandum on wardrobe offer to Doris Day, 22 March 1955. *Man Who Knew Too Much* Casting file 377, Alfred Hitchcock Collection, HER.

Coleman, Herbert, Letter to Alfred Hitchcock regarding the Dar es-Salam, nd. *Man Who Knew Too Much* Location file 387, Alfred Hitchcock Collection, HER.

———, Personal correspondence, 13 July 1995.

———, Personal correspondence, 19 July 1995.

Davenport, Guy, *The Geography of the Imagination* (San Francisco: North Point, 1981).

Day, Doris, Personal communication, 25 August 1995.

De Beauvoir, Simone, *The Second Sex*, trans. Constance Borde and Sheila Malovany-Chevallier (New York: Alfred A. Knopf, 2009; first published 1949).

Duker, Vernon, Personal correspondence, 8 September 1995.

Durkheim, Émile, *The Division of Labor in Society* (New York: Macmillan, 1933).

Erickson, Clarence O., 'Doc', Letter to Frank Caffey regarding Marrakech production, 6 May 1955. *Man Who Knew Too Much* 1955 Production file 12, Paramount Production Records, HER.

———, Letter to Frank Caffey regarding Marrakech production, 19 May 1955. *Man Who Knew Too Much* 1955 Production file 12, Paramount Production Records, HER.

———, Letter to Hugh Brown regarding Marrakech, 21 May 1955. 1955 Production file 12, Alfred Hitchcock Collection, HER.

———, Letter to Frank Caffey regarding Albert Hall and other shooting, 7 June 1955. 1955 Production file 12, Paramount Production Records, HER.

Forest, Carl, Personal communication, 30 August 1995.

Frankel, Marty, Personal communication, 5 February 2016.

Frazer, James George, *Totemism and Exogamy: A Treatise on Certain Early Forms of Superstition and Society* (London: Macmillan, 1910).

Freccero, John, '*Blow-up*: From the Word to the Image', in Roy Huss (ed.), *Focus on Blow-up* (Englewood Cliffs, NJ: Prentice-Hall, 1971), pp. 116–28.

Friedan, Betty, *The Feminine Mystique* (New York: Dell, 1963).

Gélin, Daniel, Personal correspondence, 21 November 1995.

Halberstam, David, *The Fifties* (New York: Ballantine, 1993).

Hartwright, G. G., Letter to Rev. J. F. Balley, St Saviour's Church, Brixton Hill, regarding belfry repair, 13 May 1955. Greater London Record Office.

Hayes, John Michael, Personal communication, 23 October 1994.

Hayman, Irene, Personal correspondence, 26 July 1995.

Hitchcock, Alfred, 'The Core of the Movie – The Chase', in Sidney Gottlieb (ed.), *Hitchcock on Hitchcock: Selected Writings and Interviews* (Berkeley: University of California Press, 1995), pp. 125–32.

———, 'Films We Could Make', in Sidney Gottlieb (ed.), *Hitchcock on Hitchcock: Selected Writings and Interviews* (Berkeley: University of California Press, 1995), pp. 165–8.

Kynaston, David, *Austerity Britain: 1945–51* (London: Bloomsbury, 2008).

———, *Family Britain: 1951–57* (London: Bloomsbury, 2010).

Lawrence, D. H., *Studies in Classic American Literature* (Garden City, NY: Doubleday, 1953).

Livingston, Jay, Personal communication, 18 September 1995.

Luraschi, Luigi, Inter-Office Communication to Alfred Hitchcock regarding Burmese censorship, 5 September 1957. Distribution file 384, Alfred Hitchcock Papers, HER.

Man Who Knew Too Much, The, file, Motion Picture Association of America, Production Code Administration Records, HER.

———, Dubbing file 385, Alfred Hitchcock Papers, HER.

———, Herbert Coleman 1955 file 379, Alfred Hitchcock Papers, HER.

———, Production 1955–6 file 391, Alfred Hitchcock Papers, HER.

May, Elaine Tyler, *Homeward Bound: American Families in the Cold War Era* (New York: Basic Books, 2008).

Pomerance, Murray, 'Finding Release: "Storm Clouds" and *The Man Who Knew Too Much*', in James Buhler, Caryl Flinn, and David Neumeyer (eds), *Music and Cinema* (Middletown, CN: Wesleyan University Press, 2000), pp. 207–46.

———, 'Looking up: Class, England, and America in *The Man Who Knew Too Much*', in Jonathan Freedman (ed.), *The Cambridge Companion to Alfred Hitchcock* (New York: Cambridge University Press, 2015), pp. 180–93.

Ritchie, Rachel. '"Beauty isn't all a matter of looking glamorous": Attitudes to Glamour and Beauty in 1950s Women's Magazines', *Women's History Review* vol. 23 no. 5 (2014), pp. 723–43.

Said, Edward W., *Orientalism* (New York: Vintage, 1979).

———, *Culture and Imperialism* (New York: Vintage, 1994).

Showalter, Elaine, *The Female Malady: Women, Madness, and English Culture, 1830–1980* (New York: Pantheon, 1985).

Simmel, Georg, 'On Visual Interaction', in Robert E. Park and Ernest W. Burgess, *Introduction to the Science of Sociology* (Chicago: University of Chicago Press, 1921), pp. 356–60.

Truffaut, François, *Hitchcock*, trans. Helen Scott (New York: Simon & Schuster, 1984; rev. edn).

Weis, Elisabeth, *The Silent Scream: Alfred Hitchcock's Sound Track* (Madison, NJ: Fairleigh Dickinson University Press, 1982).